D1713130

To Harry N. Roberts --

With deep appreciation for your significant contribution to this book. No one could have presented the information more clearly.

Jack Brosius

Dave Eby

Canoes&Kayaks:
A COMPLETE BUYER'S GUIDE

Nov. 15, 1979.

Canoes&Kayaks:
A COMPLETE BUYER'S GUIDE

JACK BROSIUS and DAVE LEROY

cbi Contemporary Books, Inc.
Chicago

Library of Congress Cataloging in Publication Data

Brosius, Jack.
    Canoes and kayaks.

    Bibliography: p.
    Includes index.
    1. Canoes and canoeing. 2. Boating industry—
North America. I. LeRoy, Dave, 1920—
        joint author. II. Title.
VM353.B77   623.82′9   78-21576
ISBN 0–8092–7691–7
ISBN 0–8092–7690–9 pbk.

Copyright © 1978 by Trend Books, Inc.
Published by Contemporary Books, Inc.
180 North Michigan Avenue, Chicago, Illinois 60601
Manufactured in the United States of America
Library of Congress Catalog Card Number: 78-21576
International Standard Book Number: 0-8092-7691-7 (cloth)
                                     0-8092-7690-9 (paper)
Published simultaneously in Canada by
Beaverbooks
953 Dillingham Road
Pickering, Ontario L1W 1Z7
Canada

We dedicate this book to the American and Canadian designers, testers, builders, and sellers of canoes and kayaks—two of mankind's most ancient forms of transportation which are nevertheless as modern as tomorrow morning's newspaper.

Contents

Foreword

This is the second book about canoes and kayaks that we have coauthored for the same publisher. The first one told how to build and repair fiberglass canoes and kayaks. This one is quite different. It is, in effect, a sizable sales catalog—covering the products, canoes and kayaks, of more than 70 manufacturers and the equipment and accessories that go with those canoes and kayaks. (The companies are located from coast to coast in the United States and in various cities of Canada.)

It is also a good bit more than that.

The copy and the manufacturers' pictures that have been selected are, quite frankly, presented in a way that we hope will motivate you to make your choice and go out and buy. For this we offer no apologies. Paddling is great fun and wonderful exercise. And where else can you find a vehicle that will serve so well and so long at such a low upkeep?

We believe that the early chapters will "prep" you well on canoe and kayak designs and their uses and on the complexities of modern-day construction. Such information is vital to making an intelligent choice.

We have also devoted considerable space to accessories—and especially to those that are important for propelling the canoe or kayak, for the safety of the occupants, and for overall enjoyment.

The chapter on used equipment is, we believe, a complement that no book of this type should be without. There are many good buys in used canoes and kayaks, but there are also hazards—including the possibility that the "steal" you find will be precisely that, a stolen boat. What to watch out for—as regards damage, flaws, and legal ownership—is discussed in detail.

You will note that some of the boats and accessories listed herein have suggested retail prices and that some do not. Usually, prices are omitted because the manufacturer did not include them along with sales literature, catalog, and pictures. In a few instances, they have been omitted for mechanical reasons. In a few other instances, they have been left out because the manufacturers indicated to us that they would go up before the book could be in print.

Fuel shortages and general inflation can make prices obsolete pretty rapidly these days, and it is obvious that some readers will on occasion encounter prices higher than those quoted herein.

However, whatever you're in the market for, we are convinced that the intelligent use of this book will save you more than its price—in dollars alone, not to mention time, trouble, and driving costs.

Arlington, Virginia

Jack Brosius
Dave LeRoy

Picture Credits

All of the interior photographs and drawings are by manufacturers or their agents unless they have been otherwise credited.

Glossary

You will want to remember the meanings of the following terms when you are reading this book and manufacturers' literature.

Beam: The width of a canoe or a kayak at its widest point.

Blade: The paddle section which goes into the water; may be straight or scooped.

Freeboard: The distance from the normal waterline to the bottom of the gunwale.

Gunwales: Wood or metal strips along the top sides of a canoe, extending from the bow to the stern.

Heavy water: Water of great volume with strong wave action and currents.

Inwale: The side of the gunwale facing to the inside of the boat.

Keel: A strip protruding from the hull, generally along the center of the bottom, and usually extending from the bow to the stern.

Outwale: The side of the gunwale facing away from the boat.

Portage: To carry a boat overland between waterways, usually around obstacles.

Ribs: Frames extending from gunwale to gunwale to form the shape of the hull.

Rocker: The upward curvature of the keel line of a boat from the center toward each end.

Shoe keel: A wide, shallow keel.

Sponson: A bulge in the side of a boat that helps improve stability.

Spray skirt: A device for keeping out water, which is constructed of waterproof fabric with elastic bands at the top and the bottom and is worn by the paddler and attached to the cockpit.

Stem: A piece of wood or metal at the ends of a canoe.

Stem plate: A strip of metal over the leading edge of the stem.

Swamp: To fill with water.

Thwart: A brace across a boat from gunwale to gunwale.

Tumblehome: The curvature of a canoe side from its widest point to the gunwale.

Waterline: The level of the water along the side of a boat at its designed capacity with proper weight distribution.

Yoke: A device extending across the width of a canoe that is used to facilitate portaging.

Canoes&Kayaks:
A COMPLETE BUYER'S GUIDE

1

Living in the Quiet Other World

—Down a smooth, clean river whose width is constantly changing and past an occasional island with its virgin timber. On the riverbank white-tailed deer stand wide-eyed, but they do not run.

—Onto a shore, the bow end crunching gently on the frozen ground. Beautiful birch trees rise majestically from the new-fallen carpet of snow. With the tent pitched and camp made, fire snaps merrily as the coffeepot bubbles.

—Casting off at dawn on a brackish, two-mile-wide river 50 miles from the Atlantic Ocean, and watching yard-long rockfish boil up from the water in their morning feeding.

—Portaging along the banks of a picturesque creek as the sun begins its final descent.

—Gliding swiftly down "stairsteps" in heavy whitewater, eyes glued ahead for the dark outlines of submerged rocks . . . kayak blade poised to react . . . a thrill a minute.

—Dropping anchor in late afternoon, near the shoreline of a placid lake, and breaking out the tackle for largemouth bass.

Vignettes such as the above are a sampling of the great and serene life that awaits you in the world of canoes and kayaks. Whether your sport is cruising or camping or racing or whitewatering, or some combination, these two ancient means of transport are available to serve you—and eternally please you.

In an America that turns increasingly to the highway with every passing year, the two craft—graceful, slim, sleek cousins—offer a golden opportunity to "get away from it all." They are the ticket away from urban sprawl, congested freeways, dirty air, dirty water, honking horns, persistent telephones. *Away, period!*

The canoe and the kayak have served mankind for centuries—as family vehicles, as war vessels, as fishing boats, as hunting craft, as the trucks of their eras, in commerce of many kinds, and in sport. Yet they have reached new heights of popularity in this age of jet aircraft and the broad interstate highway. Why is this so?

Every canoe and kayak presents its owner with something of a challenge. The paddler is to the boat roughly what a rider is to a spirited horse. The two are as one. There are things to be respected and things to be learned. Almost anybody can jump into a powerboat, pull the starter cord on the outboard motor, and go blasting off. The canoe and the kayak demand some finesse—but they give a lot in return for it.

They fulfill a need for exercise. Why build your biceps with barbells when a paddle will do it—and take you to magnificent vistas, far from roads and the madding crowds, in the process?

They do not require a large investment of money. A big powerboat needs a trailer, auxiliary tags, lighting and braking, gasoline, oil, and perhaps a rental slip in a marina. Not so the canoe or the kayak. It will travel on an inexpensive cartop carrier. Its gear consists mainly of paddles, lifejackets, and helmets.

Canoes and kayaks are shallow-draft. They can go almost wherever there is water, even in times of drought.

Maintaining a canoe or a kayak is easy. With reasonable care, either will last a lifetime.

They are light—some are very light—and therefore easy to pull from the water and to portage around obstacles. Despite that fact, they have excellent hauling capacity—often ten times their weight or more.

Propelling a canoe is not limited to paddling. Whether square-sterned or double-pointed, it can be pushed along by a low-horsepower outboard motor. It can also be sailed or poled.

Today, the two craft are the products of the best design work and construction materials and techniques in their long histories. They have undergone rigid testing for performance, for safety, and for durability.

They are still popular in canvas over wood and in other forms of wood. Aircraft and marine technology have combined to turn out top-quality aluminum boats. Fiberglass boatbuilding has advanced by leaps and bounds. And new, sophisticated materials such as Kevlar and Royalex are in use for hulls and reinforcement.

Never before have canoeists and kayakers had such choices.

But the technology of the late '70s has not taken away the ancient virtues of canoes and kayaks—especially utility, simplicity, economy, versatility, and durability. Indeed, it has added to those virtues.

The two craft were, among other things, the equivalent of the family auto to the American Indian, and they can be just as useful to the modern family that wants to do its water sports and its shoreline camping together.

"Age 8 to 80 and anywhere in between" is the way the canoe industry describes the broad appeal of its products.

The pictures on the following pages depict some of the fun. The extensive survey of American and Canadian manufacturers shows the variety of choices.

2
Designs and Their Uses

It is easy to become confused and discouraged when shopping for a new canoe or kayak because the buyer must choose from several classifications and a variety of construction materials. The confusion over classifications is compounded by the fact that there is no standardization of boat types by manufacturers. Manufacturer A may advertise a given boat for racing, but Manufacturer B may have a very similar craft that he designates for cruising. And Manufacturer C may not bother to classify his boats at all.

This chapter seeks to clarify the picture by explaining all the characteristics of today's boats. The reader should also consult Chapter 3 for additional information about construction materials and building techniques.

Canoes are either open (undecked) or closed (decked). Kayaks are always decked.

A decked canoe looks very much like a kayak. The kayak, however, is the narrower of the two, and it is therefore usually lighter.

The Classes

Basically, there are three classes of canoes and kayaks: cruising, racing, and cruising-racing. There is also a class of sailing canoes.

Cruising canoes and kayaks are generally designed to hold two to four people and the food and gear that are needed to maintain those people for four or five days of river cruising. Cruising canoes and kayaks come in many shapes and forms and have many origins. Their usual length is from 13 to 18 feet, and their usual beam width is from 32 to 36 inches.

Cruising canoes and kayaks in the United States trace their designs to those used by fur trappers and traders and Indians, who plied the rivers and lakes with their cargo. These boats normally have pointed bows and sterns. Their bottoms are flat, except for the more sophisticated boats with added rounding of hulls. They have seats, and are comfortable for long or short trips.

Decked cruising canoes derive from racing slalom canoes, and are designed to be fast and maneuverable.

New paddlers sometimes become intrigued by the "hot" racing kayaks and buy them for cruising. This is a serious mistake. Such kayaks are low on stowage capacity and uncomfortable on long trips.

Racing canoes and kayaks were built for speedy travel between two points. They are radical in design and they require a lot of skill to operate effectively.

There are essentially four major subclasses of racing boats:

1. Olympic canoes and kayaks. These are highly specialized and are built for use on flat water. Most are constructed in Europe to meet international standards.

2. Canoes and kayaks built to International Canoe Federation standards for downriver or slalom types. A downriver 15-foot boat is very pointed and narrow and very fast. It does not have good maneuverability, but it does not need it. A slalom boat for one person is usually 13 feet long; for two persons, 15 feet long. Slalom boats for two persons are dubbed "C-2s" (C for canoe and 2 for two people). Both types are very fast, and highly maneuverable for turning through gates.

3. Marathon racing canoes and kayaks. These meet the United States Canoe Association's specifications for marathon racing. They are light, exacting in design, and built for high performance. They demand great technique in paddling and are not for the every-now-and-then user. Their shallow hulls are not built to carry much cargo.

4. A new class—the open canoe for whitewater racing. The beams of these canoes are about 30 to 36 inches wide, and the canoes are very stable. Being undecked, canoes of this kind are very roomy and can handle lots of cargo. They are significantly faster than cruising canoes.

Cruising-racing canoes and kayaks are either cruising boats modified to make them fast enough for racing, or racing designs modified to add enough stability and volume to make them pleasurable for cruising. Both types seek to satisfy the human appetite for speed and agility.

Canoe sailing can be done with any canoe that is rigged for it. For the rigs and how they work, see Chapter 5.

The Materials

Canoes and kayaks are now manufactured in aluminum, fiberglass, Kevlar, ABS plastic, Royalex plastic, canvas over wood, and wood strips.

The most extensively used material for cruising canoes is aluminum. Six to eight major U.S. manufacturers build aluminum boats. These manufacturers use some of the technology employed in aircraft construction, forming the metal and riveting it together. Though the designs used by the various manufacturers are not identical, they are similar, so that there are no significant paddling differences between comparable boats of different make.

Most aluminum boats have flotation chambers fore and aft. Some have keels, and some do not. There are variations in metal thicknesses and in construction techniques.

Metal thicknesses should be considered because of their effect on the craft's weight. If your canoe will travel only a few feet from cartop to water, a difference of five to ten pounds can be disregarded. If you have a long trip from cartop to water, or if you expect to do a lot of portaging, weight becomes important.

Most fiberglass boats are built by one of two methods. In the chopped-fiber-and-spray-up method, a gel (outer) coat is sprayed into the mold; fiberglass cloth is then added, and thickness is built up with chopped fiber and resin. In the hand-layup method, the gel coat is built, and then successive layers of fiberglass cloth, and sometimes the material known as woven roving, are added.

Vacuum molding is a third method of building in fiberglass. This expensive process puts a premium price on boats. Boats built by vacuum molding are very light in weight.

A fiberglass boat will generally be about equal in weight to an aluminum boat of the same length and beam. This is not true, however, of fiberglass boats that are Kevlar-reinforced. These boats are superlight, and most of them are made only for racing. Few, if any, cruising canoes contain Kevlar.

Boats of ABS plastic or Royalex plastic are built by means of a special molding process that forms the hull (and the deck, if there is one) as one unit. Such boats are very strong and very impact-resistant, but they present a problem when they are punctured.

Canvas-over-wood canoes and kayaks grow scarcer with the years. They are entirely hand-built, employing construction tech-niques that date back to 1908–10. The amount of hand labor required to build them makes them expensive. They are fairly light, but they will gain weight over a season of use if their wood is not kept well varnished.

In the U.S. Midwest, where marathon rac-ing has become very popular, canoes built of cedar strips and with fiberglass skins are the most prevalent. Canoes and kayaks built for marathon use also come in all of the other usual materials except ABS and Royalex.

Canoes and Kayaks—
How and of What They're Built

To make a good buy in a canoe or a kayak, you need to know as much as possible about how it was built and about the materials that were used to build it. Then, by comparing those methods and materials with the methods and materials used to build other canoes or kayaks, and by studying the specifications, you can make your decision.

After a lot of reading, you may be tempted to go out and buy a boat built of "exotic" materials, such as Kevlar or ABS plastic, because of the many wonderful things that have been written about those materials. That is not the way to judge whether a particular canoe or kayak is for you. Rather, the test should be: *What do you like best*, considering materials and all other factors, including price and expected use? Using that test, you might wind up with a boat of aluminum, fiberglass, wood, or something else.

Should you make a mistake, you can sell your boat and buy another. Used canoes and kayaks are in demand, and you are not likely to encounter really sharp depreciation, such as you would take on an automobile.

Or perhaps—as your interest in paddling grows—you will find that no one boat can fit into all your plans, and you will eventually own two or three or more. If that happens, fine. After all, canoes and kayaks are not very expensive, and they are easy to store and cheap to maintain.

As was noted in the preceding chapter, aluminum is today's most prevalent material for cruising canoes. The manufacturers of cruising canoes form and assemble them in much the same way—but, as you will read later, this statement is not meant to imply that there are no important differences among brands and models.

Fiberglass boats are built in varying ways, but in general the process is as follows: First, the builder creates what is in effect a boat mock-up. This is known in the trade as a

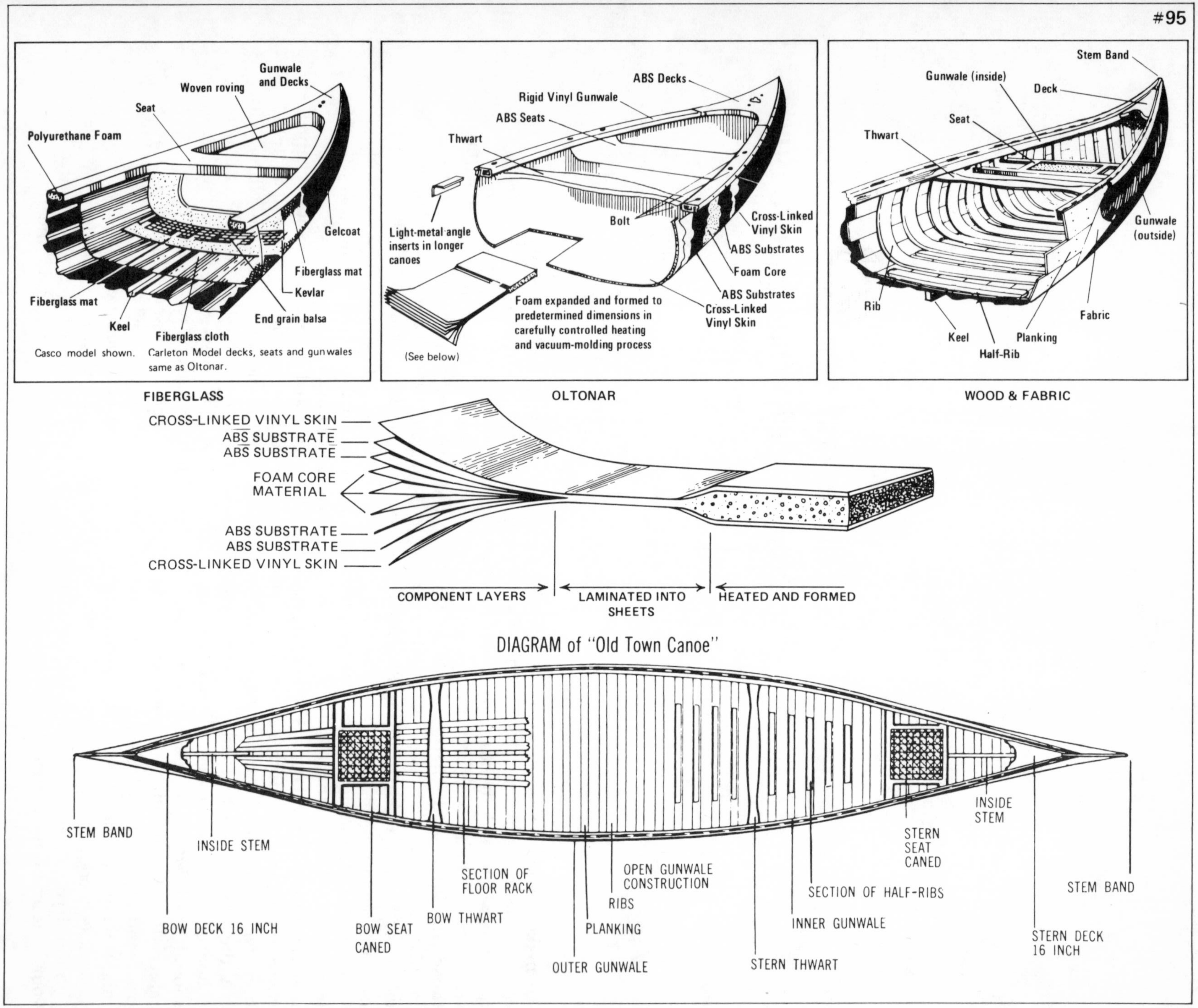

#95

WOOD & FABRIC

Stem Band
Gunwale (outside)
Deck
Gunwale (inside)
Fabric
Seat
Planking
Half-Rib
Thwart
Keel
Rib

FIBERGLASS

Gunwale and Decks
Gelcoat
Woven roving
Fiberglass mat
Kevlar
Seat
End grain balsa
Polyurethane Foam
Fiberglass cloth
Fiberglass mat
Keel
Fiberglass mat

Carleton Model decks, seats and gunwales same as Oltonar.

Casco model shown.

ABS Decks
Rigid Vinyl Gunwale
ABS Seats
Thwart
Cross-Linked Vinyl Skin
ABS Substrates
Foam Core
ABS Substrates
Cross-Linked Vinyl Skin
Bolt
Foam expanded and formed to predetermined dimensions in carefully controlled heating and vacuum-molding process
Light-metal angle inserts in longer canoes
(See below)

OLTONAR

COMPONENT LAYERS → LAMINATED INTO SHEETS → HEATED AND FORMED

CROSS-LINKED VINYL SKIN
ABS SUBSTRATE
ABS SUBSTRATE
FOAM CORE MATERIAL
ABS SUBSTRATE
ABS SUBSTRATE
CROSS-LINKED VINYL SKIN

DIAGRAM of "Old Town Canoe"

STEM BAND
STERN DECK 16 INCH
INSIDE STEM
STERN SEAT CANED
SECTION OF HALF-RIBS
INNER GUNWALE
STERN THWART
OPEN GUNWALE CONSTRUCTION
RIBS
PLANKING
OUTER GUNWALE
SECTION OF FLOOR RACK
BOW THWART
BOW SEAT CANED
INSIDE STEM
BOW DECK 16 INCH
STEM BAND

Diagrams by Old Town provide cross-section views of how the company's fiberglass, Oltonar, and wood and fabric canoes are built.

"plug." From the plug a cavity mold is created, and from the cavity mold many boats are made. For a kayak or a decked canoe, there is a separate mold for the deck, which is later joined to the hull.

The mold is carefully built and finished. The plug is coated with a release agent so that the mold will come off. The first layers of the mold are made of hard, shrink-resistant resin. Then layers of fiberglass mat or woven roving are added. Stiffening ribs on the outside of the mold help it to take the abuse of producing many boats.

When the mold has been cured, layup of canoes or kayaks from it begins. With few exceptions (chiefly racing canoes), a gel (outer) coat is first sprayed in and then permitted to dry to a tacky stage. Layers of fiberglass cloth are then added, and these are wet to full saturation with a polyester resin.

Wooden canoes and kayaks come in two designs—strip boats, or "strippers," and boats made of wood planking, with ribs on the inside and covered with canvas on the outside.

The strips of strip boats are usually one-eighth or one-fourth inch thick and three-fourths inch or one inch wide. The strips are glued together and are covered with clear fiberglass cloth and clear resin, inside and outside. The beauty of these boats thus shines through; to paint one would be a desecration.

Canvas-over-wood boats are built principally by such well-known firms as Old Town in the United States and Chestnut in Canada.

To delve deeper into construction materials and methods, we are providing an extensive excerpt from an article that was first published in the April-May 1977 issue of *Wilderness Camping* magazine. It was written by the magazine's editor, Harry N. Roberts. In reprinting this article with permission, the respected Old Town Canoe Company declared: "We believe that this article should be considered as 'required reading' for anyone about to purchase a canoe."

The following excerpts from this excellent article are also by permission. Omissions are indicated by ellipses.

By Harry N. Roberts

Aluminum

All aluminum canoes bear a strong resemblance at a distance, but up close the differences are profound and meaningful.

They're formed and assembled in much the same way. Aluminum sheet (in rolls) is cut to length and stretch-formed over a male mold to create one-half of a canoe hull. For the curious, the sheet is either gripped at both ends and pulled down and around a stationary form by hydraulic rams acting through the grippers, or the sheet is restrained by the grippers and the mold moves up into it. The former method is somewhat faster and requires less manpower. Both methods do the job—and unless you can read a micrometer to the fourth decimal place, you won't detect any thinning of the material as a result of stretch-forming.

Aluminum canoes are symmetrical; one-half of a hull is all you need to have dies for. You can turn one of the halves end-for-end, and presto, there's a whole canoe! And how do you do a square stern? You chop a foot off the stern, that's how. . . . The stretch-formed hull halves are trimmed and then joined by a keel strip. Some manufacturers attach only the keel at one station, and move the shells to other stations for further work. Others prefer to attach keel, bow and stern stems, gunwales, and thwarts in one station and in one form to ensure that the hull retains its configuration. Ribs are attached at alignment. Ribs are attached at the same time in this building method.

The hull is then sprayed in the bilge area with a zinc chromate primer/etch compound, the typical gray nonslip surface is applied, and the finish is baked. After painting (perhaps before, depending on the individual factory), the canoe is tank-tested for leaks. After that, the canoe is trimmed out with seats, flotation, bulkheads, towing eye, and decals. . . .

About half of the aluminum canoe hulls made in America are fabricated of 6061-T4 alloy (~42,000 psi yield strength) that is raised in an oven to the T6 temper after stretch-forming. The other half is made of

5052 aluminum, which has a yield strength of around 29,000 psi and is *not* heat-treatable. Of course, the mill price of 5052 sheet is 10–12 cents a pound less than the mill price of 6061. A typical 17-footer's hull form *alone* requires about 34 pounds per shell half. This is subsequently trimmed to about 24 pounds and the scrap is recycled. A little basic math tells you that it costs from $6.80 to $8.16 more per hull to build with 6061—and that doesn't include the handling and capital equipment costs of tempering! In short, if you want a 6061-T6 hull, it will cost you more than a 5052 hull. If all your paddling is on a millpond, I'm sure it won't matter. If you plan to use your aluminum hull vigorously, the far higher yield strength of 6061 makes its selection mandatory.

But there's more than just the temper to consider. Aluminum is supplied to the industry in four basic thicknesses—.061 (inches), .050, .040, and .032. The "standard," as it were, is .050. The .040 stock is conventionally used for "lightweight" models, and the .061 is used by some makers for livery canoes. It's also the standard sheet thickness for ribless aluminum canoes. The .032 sheet is, to our knowledge, used only in the Alumacraft 185 CL, the darling of the aluminum class marathon paddlers, and in the Grumman lightweights. Strength is a function of thickness . . . ; all other things being equal, the thicker the sheet, the stronger the sheet.

The question *you* must answer is how much strength *you'll* need. The expert seeking ultimate performances or extremely light weight may well opt for an aluminum canoe of .032 stock. He (or she) doesn't plan to hit boulders! The wilderness tripper or whitewater buff may want the heavier "livery special," typically available only on special order—and the odds are that most dealers don't know that they're made. Most mortals find that the standard .050 or the lightweight .040 or .032 meets their needs nicely.

We might note in passing that one of the neglected virtues of the heavier sheets is that they dimple less easily and oilcan not at all, which is to say that the hull will retain its design form better. There's that word again. Design. It's something that aluminum canoes

aren't noted for, frankly. It's not easy to form aluminum into a slippery USCA cruiser hull configuration in the first place, although it's possible. The limiting factor is the ability to join the two halves of the hull economically. If you look at the bow and stern stems of the typical aluminum canoe, you'll note that they're wide and substantial and offer room to work inside and rivet. Now consider what a bow stem would have to look like for an aluminum USCA cruiser. Not too easy to manufacture, for sure—and next to impossible to rivet. You *could* weld, of course, but that's expensive, and it destroys the temper of the metal (it anneals it) in an area where strength is critical. Or you could adhesive-bond it. One company has done extensive development work with adhesive bonding, and its boats have undergone extensive, rigorous testing. It appears that adhesive bonding works, which indicates that more sophisticated hulls in aluminum will be economically feasible in the future.

What of the rest of the boat? Does the keel matter? Do the gunwales? The thwarts? The seats? The ribs? In a word, yes. The aluminum canoe is a skeleton and skin structure, and its strength is mostly in the skeleton. The exception, and it's only an "exception" in degree, is the ribless .061 canoe. If, then, the strength of the craft is in the skeleton, it behooves us to examine that skeleton with a great deal of care.

The keel of an aluminum canoe is its backbone. It's almost always an extruded 6063 aluminum section, but it can range from downright flimsy to extremely solid. Regardless of the keel configuration (shoe or T), there are several methods of joining the shell halves of the hull to the keel. Standard practice is to place the keel in a jig, lay a neoprene gasket on top of it, position the shell halves on top of the gasket, put a plate over the whole thing, and rivet the assembly. Another method is to double the shell halves over the gasketed keel and then to rivet the assembly. This, of course, is the lightest method.

A more complex assembly, and probably the optimum for strength and stiffness, is one that involves a slotted extrusion and an internal cap.

Typically, 5/32-inch rivets are used on 1-inch centers for the keel. Exceptions? Grumman uses 1/8-inch rivets on 5/8-inch centers; Sea Nymph uses 5/32-inch rivets on 3/4-inch centers.

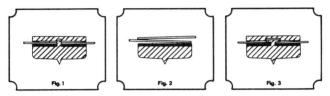

Details of the connection of keels to hull skins.
Reproduced by permission from Wilderness Camping *magazine*

As can be seen, the shell halves are fitted into gasketed slots, and the assembly is covered by an extruded cap and then riveted. The benefits are twofold. The advantages in strength and protection are obvious; less obvious is the fact that this assembly method makes it easier to build in (and maintain) a slight dead rise in the hull. The performance increase from this small amount of dead rise isn't noticeable in and of itself, but the few degrees of dead rise aid immeasurably in preventing oil-canning (hull flexing), which can hinder hull performance markedly.

Stems are usually put in place in the same station without moving the canoe, which is still a very floppy item at this point in time. Stems may be extruded 6063 or a formed 6061-T4 sheet that's heat-treated to T6 after forming. Both do the job. Stems may be riveted on 1-inch, 3/4-inch or 5/8-inch centers. While the two closer patterns are preferable, the rivet pattern is not as significant in terms of strength as is the stem configuration. At the critical point where the keel and the stem join, the stem configuration should be either slightly rounded or in a shallow vee form (and, of course, thicker as a result) to absorb grunches better. If you've ever paddled a shallow whitewater river that's heavily cruised, you'll see a lot of shiny rocks lurking underwater. Contrary to popular opinion, that glitter doesn't come from metal rubbed off keels. It comes from that part of the stem where it's joined to the keel. Look at an aluminum canoe when it's upside down on sawhorses, and your eye

will tell you where the boat will "bang" first. The meatier the stem at that point, the better.

Gunwales, decking, thwarts, and seats are all structural parts of the canoe. Flimsy gunwales and thwarts (consider seats as thwarts in terms of structural integrity) will result in a hull that's too flexible. Aluminum canoes must be stiff to minimize the skin and the rivets working against each other. Flimsy gunwales and thwarts can destroy all the good intentions of a rugged keel and rugged stems.

Ribs? Lots of ribs look sturdy, but the ribs are there primarily to maintain proper hull configuration. Certainly they add some strength—but they also act as stress risers. Ribs are usually riveted in place, though some builders use a single rivet at the end of the rib and spot-weld the rib in place. Both practices have some drawbacks. Rivets can work loose or be sheared by heavy impact, and the result is a lovely little hole or three. Spot-welds anneal the skin, and you can't toss the whole boat into an oven to retemper it because you'll destroy the keel gaskets! If you dislike either option, consider a ribless canoe, but be apprised that the ribless craft, with a skin of .061 stock and triangular bracing from the thwarts to the keel, is a *heavy* boat. . . . Look for the niceties, too. Unfinished edges under the seats and under the decks are natural-born stress risers for your hide. Too low a seat may trap your feet beneath it in an upset if you're paddling from a kneeling position. A rib in the right or wrong place, as the case may be, may make kneeling a torture, or it may provide a built-in foot brace to facilitate the stern paddler's work.

If the canoe has a bow eye for towing, it should be positioned as low as possible on the stem. Canoes neither tow well nor line well if the eye is at deck height. True, you can bridle the boat, with the line coming out at the waterline, but that's one more thing to hang up on a rock.

Rivets? Enough has been written on the merits of flush rivets versus roundhead rivets and about hard rivets versus soft rivets to patch hell a mile, and there isn't a pennyweight's difference between them as far as the average paddler is concerned. Flush rivets (countersunk rivets would be another appropriate name for them) offer a bit less drag, in theory, and they certainly offer a smoother surface that won't hang up on rocks as easily. The difference in drag is academic on a bluff-bowed hull with a fat keel hanging down, even the shallow "shoe" or "whitewater" keel. And some builders feel that flush rivets may work through the relatively thinner countersunk section faster than standard rivets would. However, while flush rivets offer little more than a psychological advantage, their presence almost always implies "that little something extra" that means a well-made boat. You don't *need* flush rivets any more than you *need* the impeccable walnut dash fascia on a Ferrari—but both make statements about the nature of the rest of the machine.

Hard rivets versus soft rivets? Hard rivets shear, soft rivets smear. No rivet is bombproof. If you pile a boat into a rock in a fast-moving river, something's going to give. Rivets, ribs, skin—you name it. Don't worry about hard or soft rivets.

So it turns out that our old friend the aluminum canoe is a rather complex beast when you look closely at it. There are lots of picky little details to investigate. More to the point, however, is consideration of what the aluminum canoe can and can't do for you.

The old saws are mostly true. Aluminum *is* noisy. Karl Ketter's classic epithet of "Boomalum" *does* apply. And aluminum is cold or hot depending on the weather, although this point is often exaggerated beyond its worth. After an hour in the water, *all* canoes assume ambient temperature. It's durable and essentially free from maintenance, but it's not indestructible. *No* canoe is indestructible. If you free your mind now of all notions of indestructible canoes, you stand a good chance of never destroying one. But an aluminum canoe that's well put together can take a lot of abuse for a long time. This is fortunate, because aluminum does not lend itself to easy repair in the field or in the shop if it should tear. Dings, dents, bends, and grunches are traditionally removed in the field by stomping on the poor, defenseless boat until the bends yield, more or less gracefully. It's little short of amazing to see what carnage can be undone on a riverbank by a well-shod pair of 12EE's!

The performance-oriented paddler (this does not necessarily mean the racer, by the way) has looked on the aluminum canoe as a mutt rather than a purebred. It's evident that the nature of the material and the nature of the fastening procedure do not lend themselves to sophisticated hull design, but some of the objections to the aluminum hull's poky ways can be overcome by simply buying an 18- or 18½-footer. Let's look at some canoes and see why.

Alumacraft makes its superlight CL models in 15-, 17-, and 18½-foot lengths. All measure the same (34¾ inches) at the four-inch waterline. It's common for aluminum canoes from the same builder to have identical or similar waterline dimensions, midship depths, and bow heights over this range of length, because the length of the canoe is modified in the stretch-forming process by adding a section of suitable length to the center of the male form. (Full-length forms for each length would be prohibitively expensive.) The Alumacraft 15-footer is a chunky little boat with a 34¾-inch beam at the four-inch waterline. A 15-footer built to USCA cruiser specs would have a four-inch waterline of 25⅞ inches. While that would be an admittedly skinny craft suitable only for singlehandling, the difference in waterline beams is startling. On the other hand, the 18½-footer's beam at the four-inch waterline is only 2¾ inches greater than that of the very efficient USCA cruiser. In simple terms, a 15-footer in aluminum will be a bit of a meat platter, while the same manufacturer's 18-footer will be a more efficient hull. True, the big canoes are heavier. The 15-foot Alumacraft CL, for example, weighs 56 pounds; the 18½-footer weighs 71. Grumman's lightweight 15-footer weighs 55 pounds, and its 18-footer only 67 pounds. The four-inch waterline beams are, again, the same. You buy a lot more performance, seaworthiness and load-carrying capacity for very little more weight and, as of this year's prices, for only about $40.

Fiberglass

Fiberglass canoes—more accurately, fiber-glass-reinforced plastic canoes—have been around nigh on to 20 years, a fact you'd never realize if you read most current books on canoeing, which treat the glass boat as an exotic experimental watercraft. . . . Glass technology is changing, true, and it has changed almost daily since people started building canoes out of fiberglass, but the basic technology is solid and well proven, and the inherent flexibility of the construction method permits the development of truly sophisticated watercraft.

Don't take this to mean that every glass boat is a sophisticated design. For every Jensen SSJ there are five river pigs. And not every glass boat is laid up in an optimum manner, either. For every Mad River TW Special there's a chopper-gun hideosity that would be more in its element if it were stood on end with a half-moon cut into its bilge and a Rent-A-John label on its bow.

How is a good glass boat built? Lots of ways—but let's go way back to when the boat is a gleam in a designer's eye. The design is transferred to paper, with transverse section curves drawn full size for each of many "sections." . . . After the canoe has been put down on paper, the section curves are transferred to wooden forms which are affixed, "upside down" as it were, to a *strongback,* a heavy, straight beam of suitable length laid across leveled sawhorses. The builder then lays up a wooden-strip canoe over these section forms. If the craft is to be used in the water for test, it's built as a true "stripper," and the forms are removed. If the designer is sufficiently confident—and the good ones are—the forms are left in place to add rigidity. The completed strip canoe is glassed and sanded and polished to within an inch of its life. At this point, it's a *plug,* a master form from which a mold will be made.

It's a tedious, fussy job to finish this plug; 50 hours of hand sanding is a fair estimate. Patience and persistence are probably more necessary than a high level of skill with wood. It is not prohibitively expensive in terms of material. If you have to hire it done, though, the labor costs are extravagant.

Now, there are some unscrupulous souls who (1) couldn't design a suitable canoe if their lives depended on it, (2) don't recognize the designer's stake in his creation, and (3) are too tightfisted to pay a skilled person to build a plug and too inept to build one themselves. These clowns, lovingly referred to as "pirates," simply buy a desirable canoe; strip the seats, thwarts, and gunwales; fill the holes; and use the canoe as a plug. Some of them are so invincibly ignorant that they don't brace their ripped-off plug adequately, and they wind up with a warped mold, which produces warped canoes. . . . Others add a keel—or two or three. . . .

At any rate, by means fair or foul, there's a plug. The next step is to prepare the plug with multiple coats of mold-release wax and/or PVA (polyvinyl alchohol) mold release and to lay up a mold. The first layers are, typically, of a hard, shrink-resistant tooling resin; subsequent layers are formed of mat or roving; and stiffening ribs or wooden frames may be built in. The object is a mold that's stiff, durable, and will take a lot of use (and abuse.)

After the mold has been completed, the process of laying up the canoe can begin. With few exceptions (all of them racing canoes), the process begins with a gel coat, a dense isophthalic polyester resin that's sprayed into a waxed mold in a thin layer and permitted to cure, or mostly cure. The next step is to lay up several layers of glass cloth in the mold, the thicknesses determined by the strength and weight necessitated by the design. A typical construction might be three layers of ten-ounce glass cloth, or two layers of ten-ounce and one of six, or several other combinations that amount to essentially the same thing. The cloth is draped into the mold and wet with catalyzed polyester resin which is thoroughly rolled or worked into the cloth so that the cloth is fully saturated. Excess resin is removed by "sweeping" it over the gunwales with squeegees. The key to this operation is the care and thoroughness with which the cloth is wet and the excess resin removed.

Patches of fabric that aren't wet thoroughly will delaminate; excess resin results in a heavy, brittle boat.

Some folks cherish the myth that a glass boat is "popped out of a mold like a cookie." Nonsense. There's a lot of hand labor in a glass canoe—15 to 20 man-hours in all for a really exotic one. And a good chunk of that labor time is spent in properly wetting out the cloth and removing the excess resin.

After the cloth layers are laid up in the mold, the next task is to lay up additional material in the bilge to stiffen the hull. Depending on the manufacturer, this may be cloth, woven roving (a "basketweave" cloth made up of flat-laid strands), or mat (a pressed "felt" of short strands of glass). Typical good practice consists of a bilge "cookie" of lightweight mat and an inner layer of lightweight woven roving. Some folks will scream about any mat in a canoe, but mat bilge cookies are acceptable practice if: (1) the mat is not flooded with resin, (2) the mat is not excessively thick, and (3) the roving laid up over it is wet out by rolling it well into the mat to further absorb resin. Mat applied properly has a reasonable section modulus, resulting in a stiff bilge without excessive weight, and it's considerably less expensive than multiple layers of cloth, or a layer of foam, or end-grain balsa. Cloth would, of course, be the strongest bilge-stiffening layer, but it would take several layers to be stiff enough (and many more layers in critical areas for "grunch strips" and such), and as we've noted, laying up and squeegeeing out a lot of layers of cloth is expensive. For example, Mad River's impeccable TW Special has as many as *ten* layers of cloth in certain areas of the hull, which goes a long way toward explaining its list price, in glass, of $579.

Foam (Midwestern Fiberglass and 6-H) and balsa (Old Town) are used as bilge stiffeners in a limited number of canoes. Both are expensive; both require great care to ensure complete bonding. Both require an additional layer of cloth over them to prevent them from soaking up water. Both are difficult to repair; the foam is intensely difficult. . . . Both are very stiff, and result in hulls that maintain

their design configuration with a minimum of weight. Even more exotic materials—Hexcel aluminum honeycomb and a resin-impregnated cardboard honeycomb—are used in "ultra"-competition canoe layups, usually in conjunction with vacuum bag–molded Kevlar-49 cloth and epoxy resins, but these canoes are so rare that the average paddler will never see one unless he or she attends a marathon canoe race.

So, then—good commercial practice is to lay up a canoe with several layers of glass cloth, a mat bilge cookie, and a woven roving inner layer. The result is a relatively stiff canoe that holds its configuration well even with lightweight aluminum gunwales, and yet is flexible enough to endure a lot of pounding. The all-cloth layups, which represent exceptional commercial practice, are usually a bit lighter and a bit more resilient than the norm. Neither type will take remorseless pounding, but fiberglass won't dent, there are no rivets to pop, and it's easily repaired in the field, which is a virtue neither aluminum, Royalex, nor Oltonar can claim. . . .

We must note again that there is a fair latitude in what is considered good building practice, and each builder has some idiosyncrasies in this respect. Some are in love with an internal keel strip, which may be of half-round wood, aluminum tubing chopped in half, or a half-round molded glass section. These are laid in next to the cloth and held in place with either cloth or a mat bilge cookie. They add a lot of stiffness to the hull with only minimal weight.

Some builders, notably Mike Cichanowski at Midwestern Fiberglass, are enamored of "pogo sticks," spring-loaded aluminum tubes that run from an internal keel up to the amidships thwart. The theory behind the pogo stick is that it will keep the keel rigid and maintain the hull's form easily under normal going, but permit the hull to flex freely under unusual loads. . . .

Some builders, particularly those who use the cloth, mat bilge cookie, and roving fabrication method, lay up ribs of cloth or mat that run from the bilge cookie almost to the gunwale. The idea here is to distribute some of the loading that may occur at the interface between the relatively thin freeboard area and the thicker, stiffer bilge. Again, it's not the ultimate way to build a canoe, but it's a good way if practiced by a conscientious builder. It's far too easy to let yourself be seduced by some notion of "ultimate" construction when all you need is a good, basic hull—which means that you have to analyze your needs before you buy.

Other idiosyncrasies appear in seats, gunwales, and thwarts. Aluminum extrusions pop-riveted in place make workable, durable gunwales. They lack the handsome appearance of wood, but they're less expensive, they require no maintenance, they're usually narrower so that you can get your paddle a bit closer to the keel line, they're lighter, and they don't leave splinters in your hands. Again—good commercial practice. But the folks at Old Town, who've made a lot of good canoes over the years, swear by extruded vinyl gunwales. They'll make you a canoe with aluminum rails if you ask them loudly and often, but they feel that aluminum rails will fail in such a way as to be unrepairable in the field, and may fail in such a way as to cause the canoe to tear in half. They do reinforce their extruded vinyl gunwales with aluminum L-sections in the larger canoes, but they point out that this is reinforcement and that the strength and flexibility are in the vinyl, which will wrap rather than tear. And the folks at Mad River can give you all sorts of cogent reasons for using hardwood rails: they're flexible, they're tough, the outwale can be made wide enough to act as a splash rail without incurring a tremendous weight penalty, and nothing is easier to repair in the field or in the shop. . . .

Thwarts? I like 'em—lots of 'em. Five is about right for an 18½-footer to my way of thinking, and that doesn't count the seats, which act as thwarts structurally. Again—wood is fine, and pop-riveted aluminum tube works. Some eminently respectable builders claim that too many thwarts will cause a boat to break apart with more certainty if it's wrapped around a rock and that it's better to let it wrap without impediment. That it *will*

wrap is a foregone conclusion, of course. Any canoe filled with water and broached across a rock or a deadhead or a bridge abutment in a fast current will wrap. What happens then is up to the powers that be—and the integrity of the manufacturer.

Before we leave fiberglass, however, we must take note of a certain class of glass boats. These can generally be recognized by their price—well under $200—if not by their lack of aesthetic appeal. These are the "chopper gun" boats, made of a chopped mat and polyester resin mixture which is sprayed into a gel-coated mold with a pressure gun. The result is a heavy, brittle, resin-flooded layup that has no place in the life of a paddler who aspires to more than park lake paddling. The designs are usually lackluster, and the quality of the fitting-out is defined already by the selling price. There are, regrettably, no shortcuts with fiberglass fabrication that work really well. . . .

Kevlar® 49

Kevlar® 49, a golden-yellow fiber that saw the light of day in Du Pont's laboratories in the late '60s and was introduced, prosaically enough, as Tire Cord B in 1970, is an aromatic polyamide that's generically called an aramid.

By any measurement, it's tough stuff. Composites of Kevlar® 49 have a considerably higher tensile strength and flexural modulus than composites of E-glass when laid up with the same resin systems. Impact, tear, and penetration resistances are also significantly higher.

Further, Kevlar® 49, which is available in a variety of fabric weights and weaves and in woven roving as well, has the same ability to be molded in refined shapes as glass cloth. In fact, you can consider it as another breed of glass in loose, general terms of workability—but the similarity ends there.

Kelvar® 49 has given a lot of canoe builders fits over the past four years. It's difficult to check on proper wetout because the fabric changes color very little. The fabric didn't respond well to conventional boat polyesters because they were formulated for flexibility based on the use of fiberglass cloth. And a number of early Kevlar® 49 boats had a history of delamination. Shades of the early days of another miracle fiber—fiberglass!

A lot of water has gone over Wesser Falls since then. The surface finish of Kevlar® 49 has been modified to make it more compatible with certain resin systems, which has largely ended delamination problems and "soft" boats. . . .

Kevlar is expensive stuff—approximately three times as costly as glass of comparable dimensions. It requires extreme care and craftsmanship in molding as well. The combination of these factors has made all-Kevlar canoes very expensive. The result, of course, is that a lot of the visible use of Kevlar has been in racing canoes (or, more accurately, in cruising canoes that are used in competition). This has served to give the fabric the unwarranted reputation of being useful only for ultralight "racing boats." Kevlar is, of course, admirably suited to the racer's needs. An all-Kevlar canoe is both very light and very strong. . . .

Kevlar brings out the development engineer in a lot of boatbuilders, too. Sawyer Champs and the Jensen USCA cruisers made by Ev Crozier in Kevlar and honeycomb layups with epoxy resin have come in at *under 30 pounds* fully trimmed out, and they're tough and stiff. Expensive? Better you shouldn't ask. And up in Orillia, Ontario, Pinetree Canoes, Ltd., is building its 16-foot 4-inch Ojibwa in a Kevlar and epoxy layup using vacuum bag molding to drive that last one percent of air out of the layup. The result? *Thirty-seven pounds* of very fast, very tough wilderness tripper.

There's also application for this fabric as a reinforcing layer in a glass layup. It makes an admirable grunch strip for both bow and stern, and it makes a very tough bilge cookie with a lot of stiffness. . . .

In summary, Kevlar's here to stay as a canoe material. It's not everybody's cup of tea, to be sure. If you don't need the additional toughness and the dramatic weight reduction made possible by Kevlar, there's no point in spending the many extra dollars for a Kevlar canoe. But if you need them, it's the greatest thing since sliced bread.

Vinyl—ABS—Foam Laminate

This material is a composite, a sandwich if you will, of cross-linked vinyl, acrylonitrile-butadiene-styrene sheet (ABS) and unicellular (closed-cell) foam. A typical configuration might by vinyl, ABS, ABS, foam, foam, foam, ABS, ABS, vinyl, although it must be kept in mind that different builders use different "sandwiches." There is no "standard" laminate. . . .

Each section of the laminate is there for a most specific reason. ABS sheet is readily degraded by ultraviolet radiation unless it's protected. You can protect ABS above water (and as a paddle) with an acrylic copolymer coating, but that tends to get grunched off a canoe hull over the years. Cross-linked vinyl offers good protection. ABS sheet has a lot of penetration resistance, but it's floppy. Combine it with foam, though, to add stiffness and further absorb impact, and you have a material that's exceedingly difficult to puncture. Dent? Yes. ABS sheet has an excellent memory, and the laminate will recover from a small dent. A major dent, one that deforms the foam beyond the ability of the ABS sheet to spring back, can be removed by application of heat from an industrial heat gun (*not* a propane torch, please).

There's no mystery to the strength of the foam sandwich. The foam helps, of course, but the key words to remember are *section modulus*. By separating the strength layers (the ABS), and at the same time restraining their freedom to flex independently of each other, you've created an I-beam. (Fiberglass builders who know their trade use much misunderstood glass mat as a stiffener in the bilge for much the same reason.)

Two brand names of vinyl-ABS-foam sandwich (VAFS) are in use. One is Oltonar, a laminate developed by Old Town Canoe Company and used exclusively by it; the other is Royalex, a Uniroyal product, which is used by everybody else. They are *not* identical. In fact, the Royalex used by Builder A may not be the same Royalex used by Builder B. Confusing? You bet.

A look at the fabrication techniques used for VAFS will give a clue about the nature of the differences. The sheet is furnished with the center foam layers "unblown." A chemical blowing agent (a gas producer, if you will) is triggered when the sheet is heated to about 280 degrees F, and the blowing process is essentially complete at about 305 degrees F, at which temperature the canoe is molded. Molding may be accomplished by "pushing" the material into a female mold and pushing it out by shaped hydraulic rams into the ends of the mold cavity, or by vacuum-molding, in which the heated sheet is placed over a mold, a vacuum drawn on the mold, and the material "sucked in." . . .

After the material has cooled, it's popped from the mold, the excess material trimmed off, and the canoe tricked out with gunwales, thwarts, decks (if any), and seats. The only differences you can notice between a solidly made VAFS canoe and a quick and dirty one are in the trimout details! Unless you have a big set of calipers and know where to measure, the hulls (neglecting design differences) will all look pretty much alike. The problem is that they're often substantially different. The builder buys a sheet that meets his needs—and his price point. Weight is one way to make an approximate determination of the sheet thickness and of the amount of reinforcement (additional layers of ABS and foam) built into critical areas such as the keel and the stems, but that's not a final determiner either, because different trim-out techniques can result in as much as ten pounds of difference with the same hulls. Even those big calipers won't tell the whole story, because the "backbone" of the VAFS canoe is the ABS sheet. A thicker laminate may consist of more ABS, or it may be more foam. You can't really tell by pushing up and down on an inverted hull. A good hull, be it aluminum, glass, Kevlar, wood, polypropylene, or VAFS, will not be soft and floppy—but the rigidity of a VAFS hull may, again, be derived from lots of foam and comparatively little ABS.

So—you're left in the long run with only these intangibles to work with. Is the boat trimmed out well and strongly? Good. The schlock builder doesn't spend money doing a good job of trimout, because it's expensive if it's done well. Does the manufacturer build in other materials, glass, for example, and are those boats well made? What is the reputation of the boat with serious paddlers? Be wary of this, by the way. The serious paddler is often inclined to rate a canoe purely on performance, and may be oblivious to the niceties of construction. I've been guilty of this myself! And finally, consider the cost of the boat. In general, the dollars you spend for a canoe are directly proportional to its quality, and if you don't believe that, you haven't looked closely at a lot of canoes!

Now that you've found that VAFS boat, what can you expect from a good one? Expect it to be exceptionally durable, for one. ABS has an excellent "memory"; unicellular foam has excellent energy-absorbing properties; vinyl will scratch, but rarely all the way through to the ABS layers. . . .

Don't expect an unusually lightweight boat. A VAFS canoe may weigh more or less than a comparable canoe in glass, but the material isn't startlingly lightweight. Don't expect a VAFS canoe to be a nickel rocket in slackwater either. Much progress has been made in refining entry lines, but the material resists the small-radius bends that are achievable with glass, for example. And don't expect a VAFS canoe to have sufficient flotation for whitewater. The material is buoyant, true, but whitewater runners are advised to augment the flotation with foam blocks or air bags. . . .

Wood

Wooden canoes haven't largely vanished from the scene because they're "weaker" or "inferior." They've been relegated to the status of collector's items by cost alone. As energy costs increase and petrochemical costs soar through the roof, though, the time may well come when wood is once more in the economic ball park. That's fine by me. Because if they're any good at all, wooden canoes are stiff and naturally buoyant, and wood is a material that is capable of being worked in wondrously subtle ways. . . . The traditional rib-and-plank canoe is built from the inside out over a form. The stems are attached to the keel, and ribs (preformed by steaming) are attached to the keel and to the inwales, which are, in turn, attached to the stems. The canoe is then planked, and the planking is clinch-nailed to the ribs.

The hull is then covered—with glass in some instances or, traditionally, with canvas. There are several ways to canvas a canoe. The most used way is to hang the canoe in a canvas "hammock," as it were, and to draw the canvas up from both sides and tack it to the inwale. The excess fabric is trimmed. The fabric is then treated with a sealer/filler compound, and the canoe is left to cure for several weeks, after which the hull is outfitted with outwales, decks, thwarts, seats, and keel (if any), and, of course, the exterior finish is applied and the interior and trim are varnished. After all of this, stem bands are affixed, and the canoe is ready to go.

As is evident, that's a *lot* of handcrafting and a lot of storage space used while you're waiting for something to dry . . . , which goes a long way toward explaining the cost of a rib-and-plank canoe.

The materials themselves are costly, too—but you can build a relatively low-cost boat if you're willing to cut corners. For example, you can use three-inch-wide clear white cedar ribs set one-half inch or one-inch apart, or you can use two-inch-wide ribs of common grade white cedar set six inches apart. You can plank with clear red or white cedar in long sections and cut carefully to fit, or you can plank with short sections of common and be a bit sloppy with your fitting. You can rail the boat with white ash or mahogany—or you can rail it with pine. You can deck it with mahogany—or you can deck it with plywood. You can cover it with heavy canvas, fill it with a slow-setting flint paste, sand it lovingly, paint the hull with a couple of coats of good quality paint, and varnish the wood with a couple of coats of good, high-density polyurethane finish or marine spar—or you can cover it with cheesecloth; fill it with a quick-setting, brittle goo, and spray the wood with one coat of thinned varnish. You can use brass fasteners, or you can use steel fasteners—and that's one price difference *you* can check on at your local hardware store.

The cumulative differences add up. At the low end, you can buy an 18-foot rib-and-plank, canvas-covered canoe off the shelf for around $400. At the top end, you can buy an instant heirloom from Old Town, its Guide 18, in canvas with extra half-ribs, rub rails, full-length stem band and floor rack for $1,255 plus tax and shipping, and if you're lucky you'll only wait two months to get it. Somewhere in the upper middle of the price spread, Chestnut's 18-footer in the Ogilvy series, the Dave, will set you back $764 at the factory, and its 18-footer in the Prospector series, the Voyageur, a mere $687.

If you're looking to buy a stripper or a rib-and-plank canoe, you're obviously one of those people who looks on a canoe as more than a platform for fishing or a means of transporting your body and your gear from Point A to Point B. Rational discourse about relative fragility, high cost, and increased maintenance isn't going to mean much to you. There's a bit of magic in any canoe, but the wooden boat is all magic—and *that,* my friends, is what it's all about.

Polyethylene

Polyethylene has been used for kayak construction for several years, but it's just now finding its way into the canoe market under Coleman's trade name of Ram-X and Keewaydin's trade name of K-Tek. The material is a pelletized resin blended with ultraviolet inhibitors and heat stabilizers. It's formed into an extruded sheet of about 0.220-inch thickness that's vacuum-molded at about 350 degrees F. At this temperature, the material is sufficiently plastic to creep into the stems and the keel area, making the stems and keel somewhat thicker (about 0.250 inches), stiffer, and stronger.

Strength, though, doesn't seem to be a major problem with polyethylene. The material is tough, and it has excellent impact resistance and memory. It scratches easily, though, and in uninhibited form has a tendency toward surface crazing. The addition of ultraviolet inhibitors has cleared up this problem, but some of the early rotomolded kayaks would craze after long exposure to sunlight.

The material is promising; it is inexpensive and durable, and it can be molded into very sophisticated shapes. Unfortunately, the molding equipment is very expensive, as are the metal molds required, which means that it may be some time before true special-purpose craft will appear in this material. . . .

Meanwhile, all of the available data indicate that linear polyethylene is tough stuff indeed and that it can be molded in complex shapes. We'd also like to point out that this is a different polyethylene, with properties different from those of the polyethylene that is commonly used in the rotational molding of kayaks. The rotomolding process requires the use of a cross-linked high-molecular-weight material that is less rigid and is not suitable for the construction of open canoes.

4

Boats—A Detailed Look at the Market

This chapter is by far the longest of this book, and it will be the one most often referred to. The chapter presents canoes, kayaks, and a few miscellaneous boats, such as inflatables, that are made all over the United States, in Canada, and in some European countries.

The commentary on each boat is our own. The specifications have been sent to us at our request. A number of the manufacturers listed make, or have made for them under contract, accessory equipment that could not be covered. To learn about all of the equipment and about the many features and extras they offer, write them for their catalogs.

The suggested retail list prices quoted are, in most instances, the f.o.b. prices. "Wrap charges," or packaging charges, are often added, as are transportation costs and applicable sales taxes.

A special situation applies to Canadian-made boats, whose manufacturers normally quote Canadian prices. George W. Birch,

president of the old-line Chestnut Canoe Compay, Ltd., in Oromocto, New Brunswick, noted in a letter to us: "We are also enclosing suggested retail prices, f.o.b. Oromocto in Canadian funds. U.S. prices would be about 15 percent less than Canadian prices in U.S. funds, plus transportation cost." Moreover, the information received from Chestnut's shows that its prices mean "packaged for shipment" with Canadian federal sales taxes included.

The relative value of the U.S. and Canadian currencies can change, of course; transportation costs and import duties also enter the picture. Obviously, Americans living closest to Canadian points of manufacture will pay the least in transportation charges.

We believe that the specifications listed herein are in general comparable. The boat depths given are at centerline. Most manufacturers specify that the weight capacities furnished conform to the standards of the Boating Industry Association (BIA). A few decline to furnish capacities because of claims made that they feel are unfair to their boats.

The importance of this chapter is enhanced by the very special place in history that the canoe and the kayak occupy. No one we know of has described the canoe's role better than Grumman Boats: "America's lakes and rivers and streams are steeped in history and well worth exploring. The most reliable craft from which to explore, fish, and hunt these waterways is the most American craft of all—the canoe. Canoe design has evolved over thousands of years of recorded history. It developed here in North America as a workboat made from natural materials, and it remains the most efficient water craft ever designed."

The listings that follow are arranged alphabetically.

ALCAN MARINE PRODUCTS
158 Sterling Road
Toronto, Ontario, Canada M6R 2B8
Phone: (416) 531-9911

Alcan is a Canadian producer of canoes, prams, cartop boats, and outboard runabouts. It builds both aluminum and fiberglass canoes. Its aluminum canoes come in two categories of construction, a standard unit for normal cruising on lakes and rivers and a heavier-duty model for whitewater cruising. The standard model consists of stretch-formed, heat-treated aluminum alloy, with stiffeners (ribs) and an aluminum keel. Addi-

tional stability in rough water is provided by an exterior longitudinal rib along the sides just above the waterline.

The whitewater models are similar in construction to the standard models, but are provided with a flat keel in lieu of the V-shaped keel, extra ribs, and reinforcing in the bottom.

The fiberglass models, available in red or green, are of spray-up construction with aluminum gunwales and thwarts.

Flotation for all boats is provided by foam in chambers at each end of the craft.

BIA load capacities range from 434 pounds for the 11-foot 1-inch model to 741 pounds for the 17-foot models.

ALUMACRAFT BOAT COMPANY
315 West St. Julien Street
St. Peter, Minnesota 56082
Phone: (507) 931-1050

Alumacraft is a builder of aluminum canoes, bass boats, and fishing boats. Its canoes come in ten models, ranging in length from 15 feet to 18 feet 5 inches and in widths from 35½ inches to 37¼ inches.

Construction is of stretch-formed 6061 marine aluminum alloy and extruded keel and gunwales. The hull is formed in two layers and is then spot-welded and riveted together along the keel. All models except the QT-17 WWR Quetico have center thwarts that are designed to serve as carrying yokes. All models have foam flotation in sealed bulkheads at each end of the craft.

Alcan Marine Products

	Aluminum Canoes				Fiberglass Canoes	
	Cree S-11	Algonkin S-15 Whitewater W-15	Chippewa SS-16	Ojibwa S-17 Whitewater W-17	Huron 14' 2040	Huron 16' 2041
Length	11'1''	15'	16'	17'	14'	16'
Beam	38''	36''	37½	37½	34''	36''
Hull depth	12''	12''	12''	12''	14.5''	16''
Weight	45 lb	70 lb	80 lb	76 lb	75 lb	90 lb
BIA maximum load capacity	434 lb	611 lb	679 lb	741 lb	465 lb	730 lb
Price	$395	$440	$480	$460	$350	$400

The seventeen-foot Quetico cruising canoe, by Alumacraft.

The QT-15C Quetico is basically a 15-foot cruising canoe that has been designed for use on lakes and rivers, though it would probably be quite suitable for mild whitewater (up to two-foot standing waves) with just one person aboard.

The QT-17 W Quetico is a 17-foot model which features a deeper keel than the other Alumacraft canoe models. This helps give it directional stability under windy conditions.

The 17-foot-long QT-17 CL Quetico is similar to the QT-17 W, except that it does not have the extra-deep keel.

The QT-17C Quetico is the basic "standard weight" model of the Alumacraft canoe line. It is designed for general, all-around use, and it has good stability and good handling characteristics.

The QT-17 WW and QT-17 WWR Quetico have been designed for use in whitewater.

They have been provided with more ribs and a shoe keel to help them withstand the abuses of whitewater canoeing. In addition, the QT-17 WWK is constructed of heavier gauge. (0.060 inches) aluminum for additional impact resistance. The QT-17 WWK is a bit heavy for the weekend paddler who only uses his canoe on lakes and smooth rivers. However, it is an ideal canoe for people who participate in "cruising" races in which the boats are generally subjected to bumps and scrapes against rocks and other obstacles.

The QT-185 CL Quetico is a lightweight 18-foot 5-inch version of the QT-185 C. Designed to fill the need of the racing-cruising enthusiast, it has two additional ribs for strength. The capacity of the QT-185 C makes this boat a good one for trips lasting up to a week. However, an 18-foot boat is not very maneuverable, and one should take that

Alumacraft Boat Company

Model	Center Length	Maximum Beam	Maximum Depth	BIA Rated Capacity	Approximate Weight	Price
QT-15 C Quetico (standard weight)	15'	35½"	23½"	595 lb	63 lb	$339
QT-17 W Quetico (wilderness)	17'	36"	23½"	735 lb	64 lb	NA
QT-17 CL Quetico (lightweight)	17'	36"	23½"	735 lb	64 lb	$359
QT-17 C Quetico (standard weight)	17'	36"	23½"	730 lb	73 lb	$359
QT-17 WW Quetico (whitewater)	17'	36"	23½"	730 lb	76 lb	$369
QT-17 WWR Quetico (rugged whitewater)	17'	36"	23½"	730 lb	83 lb	$385
QT-17 SS (square stern)	17'2"	36¾"	23½"	810 lb	85 lb	NA
QT-185 CL Quetico (lightweight)	18'5"	36¾"	23½"	795 lb	71 lb	$379
QT-185 C Quetico (standard weight)	18'5"	36¾"	23½"	795 lb	79 lb	NA
CO-17 Camper (outboard model)	17'	37¼"	22"	820 lb	85 lb	$399

fact into consideration if a trip is planned on a narrow, twisting river.

The QT-17 SS and the CO-17 Camper are both square-stern, 17-foot canoes which are suitable for use with small outboard motors. Each of these craft weighs about 85 pounds, and although the manufacturer says that one person can cartop them, we would recommend that two people do this chore.

AMERICAN FIBER-LITE, INC.
PO Box 67
Marion, Illinois 62959
Phone: (618) 997-5474

American Fiber-Lite produces canoes, inflatable rafts, and sailboats. The canoes are fabricated in one piece from "Fiber-Lite" and the models range from the 10-foot 6-inch Pack canoe to the 17-foot 2-inch Whitewater cruising canoe. The gunwales, thwarts, and end caps are made of aluminum, and the seats are made from redwood. Also available is an optional vinyl-covered foam seat cushion with snaps for attaching it to the seat.

The Pack canoe is a one-man canoe similar to the Wee Lassie on display at the Adirondack Museum, Blue Mountain Lake, New York. It is designed to be carried by a hiker for "wilderness" trips where frequent portages have to be made or streams and rivers have to be crossed.

The Sport, also a one-man canoe, provides about twice the capacity of the Pack canoe. It can be used by two people, although the authors recommend that only one person be in it in rough water.

The Patriot is a 15-foot canoe which can be used for overnight trips on relatively calm lakes and rivers. Its length and its rather shallow depth (14 inches) make this unsuitable for long-distance cruising.

The Square Stern is a 16-foot canoe that was designed with the hunter in mind. It can be used as a standard canoe or with a small outboard motor. Due to its shallow depth (14½ inches), it is pretty much limited to day or overnight trips with two people and gear.

The keelless bottom of the 17-foot Whitewater canoe permits quick maneuvering. The craft is basically a cruising canoe with good whitewater characteristics, giving the paddler a very usable boat.

American Fiber-Lite, Inc.

Model	Length	Width	Depth	Weight	Capacity	Price
Pack	10'6"	26"	11"	29 lb	225 lb	NA
Sport	12'	33"	13"	55 lb	425 lb	$149
Patriot	15'	36½"	14"	75 lb	710 lb	$199
Square Stern	15'10"	37"	14½"	85 lb	810 lb	$289
Whitewater	17'2"	37"	14½"	87 lb	825 lb	$269

Three canoe models produced by American Fiber-Lite.

twelve-foot Sport

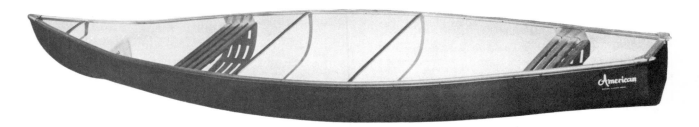

sixteen-foot Square Stern

fifteen-foot Patriot

Aqua Sport Canada, Ltd.

	12'	14'	16'4''	Vee Stern
Length	11'9''	14'	16'4''	15'6''
Beam width	42''	35''	39''	39''
Depth	13''	13''	14''	14''
Weight	50 lb	70 lb	85 lb	95 lb
D.O.T. rated capacity	530 lb	557 lb	665 lb	775 lb
Price	$240	$230	$265	$275

AQUA SPORT CANADA, LTD.
525 Champlain
Fabreville, Laval
P.Q., Canada H7P 2N8
Phone: (1-514) 625-0757

Sport Craft canoes by Aqua Sport Canada, Ltd., are of fiberglass construction, with aluminum gunwales, wooden thwarts, and cushioned, vinyl-covered seats on aluminum frames. All of these canoes have foam flotation in the bow and the stern.

The double-ended models are 12 feet, 14 feet, and 16 feet long, and the square-stern model is 15½ feet long.

Weight appears to be the major shortcoming of the Sport Craft line of canoes, with all models running about 10 to 15 pounds heavier than similar canoes. This is not too much of a problem if you do not have to carry the boat very far, and for the money, one of these canoes could be a good buy for the person who has a cottage on a lake or a river and wants a boat for pleasure or fishing.

BART HAUTHAWAY
640 Boston Post Road
Weston, Massachusetts 02193
Phone: (617) 894-1027

Wrote Carol Storrs in the July 1977 issue of the magazine *Down River:*

As a boat designer and builder, competitor, teacher and race organizer, Bart Hauthaway, 51, of Weston, Mass., has done much for the sport of paddling in the last 15 years. In the late 1950s and early 1960s, Bart was one of the founders and prime movers behind the Kayak and Canoe Club of Boston. Together with Barbara Wright and John Urban, Bart helped develop the sport in a responsible fashion.

Bart started whitewater racing in his late 30s and within a few years developed into one of the finest kayakists in the country. . . . [He was a member of] the 1965 U.S. Team that went to the World Championships and [also] won . . . many first places in New England slaloms. . . .

An avid hunter and fisherman, Bart, at first, built canoes and kayaks strictly for his own personal use. Later, he started making boats for others, and his reputation for craftsmanship spread quickly. Now, Bart designs and builds a wide range of single-person crafts, yet still takes a personal interest in everyone who comes to visit him for equipment or advice.

All Hauthaway whitewater kayaks and lightweight canoes are made of a hand laminate of fiberglass cloth in semiflexible polyester resins. The whitewater kayaks include one layer of polypropylene cloth for extra strength in the hulls.

Hauthaway is currently building four models of slalom kayaks, plus the Downriver racing model, the Downriver Touring model, the Minitouring model, and the Surf kayak. In addition to these, Hauthaway also builds six canoe models, as well as a Duck Boat and a Sneak Boat for hunting. All of these boats have two things in common: they are superbly built, and they are light.

The Slalom kayak is a "large volume" design that is suitable for both competition and recreational paddling. It is suitable for both lightweight and heavyweight paddlers, and it comes equipped with a molded seat and leg braces; a five-position, adjustable foot brace; and grab loops.

The Olympic Slalom kayak is basically a medium-volume (suitable for paddlers up to 180 pounds) competition kayak. It comes equipped with a molded seat and leg braces, a five-position foot brace, and grab loops.

The Minislalom kayak, designed for paddlers under 140 pounds, can be used for both competition and recreational paddling. It comes equipped with molded seats and leg braces; a five-position, adjustable foot brace; and grab loops.

The Junior Slalom kayak is a slalom kayak designed for the preteen (under 100 pounds) set. Its short length yet good width make this kayak a good, relatively stable boat for kids to learn in. It comes with a molded seat, foam kneepads, a five-position foot brace, and grab loops.

The Minitouring kayak is similar to the Minislalom, but it has a finer entry and deeper ends. This small-volume touring design for paddlers up to 150 pounds comes equipped with a molded seat and leg braces, a five-position adjustable foot brace, and grab loops.

The Downriver kayak is a competition boat that has been designed for "wildwater" racing. It comes equipped with a molded seat and leg braces, a five-position foot brace, and grab loops.

The Downriver Touring kayak is similar to the Downriver kayak, except that it has been provided with some "rocker" for ease in maneuverability. This is a nice boat for people who want to do lots of long-distance paddling (20 to 40 miles per day). You should be aware that these two types of boats require a little more "getting used to" than do the slalom types, but once you get used to them, you will find this a very pleasant and fast way to paddle.

The Surf kayak has been designed especially for surfing. It has a flat hull and a broad, upturned bow for easy maneuvering and to resist "diving" when the boat is riding waves. This form of kayaking should *never* be done alone or in areas where there are swimmers. The Surf is equipped with a molded seat and leg braces, a five-position foot brace, and a stern grab loop.

The 18-pound Pack canoe is an extremely lightweight, one-man canoe that has been designed to be paddled and/or carried into remote waterways. It can be propelled with either a standard canoe paddle or a kayak blade. Boxed inwales and thwarts are filled with PVC foam, and the undersides of the decks are filled with Ethafoam—all to provide good flotation. The boat is also equipped with an Ethafoam seat and grab loops.

The 32-pound Guide's Model Pack canoe and the 32-pound Hunter's canoe are the same, except that the Hunter's canoe is equipped with a gun boot and a barrel rest. Both canoes are designed primarily to be paddled by one person, but the wide beam enables these models to handle two people. To provide flotation, the inwales have been filled with PVC foam and Ethafoam has been inserted under the decks and the seat. In addition, there are grab loops both fore and aft.

The 35-pound Woods canoe is a lightweight, general-purpose craft, primarily intended for solo use but also capable of handling two paddlers with some gear. Like all the Hauthaway canoes, this craft was designed for the sportsman who "travels light." For flotation, its inwales have been filled with PVC foam and Ethafoam has been inserted under the decks. Grab loops front and rear make for ease in handling and transporting.

The 40-pound Ojibway canoe has partially covered decks and a "rockered" hull, making this a nice boat for whitewater or calm water. The Ojibway can be paddled by one or two people and can be used for slalom paddling. It is provided with fore and aft grab loops and has Ethafoam under the decks for flotation.

The 45-pound Allagash canoe is a two-man canoe designed for use on lakes, rivers, and streams by one or two people with light gear. It is equipped with front and rear grab loops, and for flotation its inwales have been filled with PVC foam and Ethafoam has been inserted under the seats and decks.

In addition to the above, Hauthaway is of-

Bart Hauthaway

Canoes

Model	Length	Width	Depth	Weight	Price
Pack	10½'	27"	10"	18 lb	$195
Guide's Model Pack	11'	33"	11"	32 lb	$260
Hunter's	11'	33"	11"	32 lb	$275
Woods	12'	32"	11½"	35 lb	$280
Ojibway	13'1½"	32"	11½"	40 lb	$320
Allagash	14'	32½"	11½"	45 lb	$325

Kayaks

Model	Length	Width	Depth	Weight	Price
Slalom	13'1½"	24"	11"	29 lb	$275
Olympic Slalom	13'1½"	24"	10½"	26 lb	$260
Minislalom	13'1½"	24"	10¼"	24 lb	$260
Junior Slalom	11'	21"	10"	21 lb	$195
Downriver	14'8"	24"	11"	30 lb	$270
Downriver Touring	14'8"	24"	11"	34 lb	$280
Minitouring	13'1½"	24"	10¼"	25 lb	$260
Surf	10½'	24"	11"	31 lb	$250

fering seven boats that show up in the price list but had not arrived in the catalog when this book was being written. These are the Giant Slalom kayak, the Touring kayak, the Greenland kayak, the 27½-pound Trail canoe, the 27½-pound Rob Roy canoe, the 36-pound Nomad Decked canoe, and the 39-pound Nomad Sailing canoe.

BLACK RIVER CANOES
Box 527
LaGrange, Ohio 44050
Phone: (216) 458-4293

Black River Canoes has been building high-quality canoes since 1964. It did not actually get into mass production until after about five years of testing its designs and its fabrication methods and materials.

All Black River canoes are of hand-layup fiberglass construction using 100 percent woven cloth, polyester resin, and a special wear-resistant gel coat both inside and outside. Gunwales are constructed of anodized marine aluminum. Flotation is provided by a foam-type material in a chamber at each end. The seats are nylon web secured to straight-grain ash frames. (Fiberglass pan-type and caned seats are also available.)

The 15 available models range in length from the 10-foot 3-inch Solo to the 18-foot Explorer and come in three different weight series—heavy, standard, and lightweight. In addition, these models are divided into pleasure craft and competition craft.

The standard series is basically the pleasure or recreational-type canoe. It consists of the Sporter, a 15-foot canoe designed for use by one or two people; the Rogue, a 16-foot model for two people and gear for camping or fishing; the Explorer, an 18-foot canoe capable of taking Mom, Pop, a kid or a pet, and camping gear for a nice weekend or a week-long trip; and the Chieftain, a 17½-foot square-stern canoe, which is designed for use with an outboard motor but can be paddled comfortably whenever the need or the desire arises.

In the lightweight series, Black River has managed to put together boats which are not only incredibly light (even for fiberglass) but are also quite handy and useful.

This series includes the Solo, a one-person canoe that has been designed to carry a 200-pound man and his hunting and fishing gear and yet be easy to "pack in." As with all boats of this type, it would be wise to get in plenty of practice without hunting and fishing gear until you get used to it. The other light-weight is the Packer, a 13-foot long canoe designed for one or two people—although two people might be pushing it a little if they are normal-sized adults. The Packer is a very good canoe for the person who does a lot of solo paddling and wants a little more boat under him than the Solo offers.

The competition or "performance" line comprises a group of canoes which have been designed for the paddler who wants a boat that he can use for competition and also take out for cruising.

This line includes the Challenger, a 17-foot canoe that fits into most "pleasure class" competition and can be used for both singles and two-man competition. This boat's widest point is just aft of (behind) the center line.

Another boat in this line is the Adventurer, an 18-foot model that weighs 75 pounds and has been designed for use on rivers, lakes, and even whitewater. The Adventurer can be used in competition one weekend and to take the family camping the next, though you should

be careful about how many people and how much gear you load into it.

The Adventurer also comes in a model called the Adventurer Flatwater. Unlike the Adventurer, this 18-foot performance canoe has no rocker. Thus, the average paddler will find it unsuitable on anything but lakes and large, smooth rivers.

Also in this line is the Scouter II (flatwater), an 18½-foot canoe designed for downriver racing and for the experienced paddler. The hull dimensions are designed to meet the USCA (United States Canoe Association) requirements for the cruising-class canoe. The hull is not symmetrical by its midship but has its maximum breadth on the four-inch waterline about 12 inches behind the midpoint but within the allowable USCA and ACA (American Canoe Association) rules for minimum drag. This canoe should be an excellent boat for the heavier two-man crew.

The Phantom is a high-performance 16½-foot C-1 (canoe for one) competition canoe built to comply with USCA and ACA rules. This boat can also be used for C-2 junior competition, and it is quite competitive when used by 150-pound paddlers.

The Lance is an out-and-out high-performance 16-foot C-1 racing-class canoe designed to create a minimum bow wave and yet have the smallest wet surface of any boat in its class. It will run at the same speed with the

Black River Canoes

Model	Length	Width	Depth	Weight Less Seats	Rec. Capacity	Price
15'6" Special	15'6"	34½"	12"	79	600	$229
Standard						
Sporter	15'	35"	11½"	55 lb.	550 lb.	$299
Rogue	16'	35½"	12¼"	63 lb.	675 lb.	$325
Explorer	18'	36½"	13"	73 lb.	850 lb.	$365
Chieftain	17'6"	36½"	13"	85 lb.	775 lb.	$385
Lightweight						
Solo	10'3"	29"	10½"	22 lb.	205 lb.	$199
Packer	13'	34"	11¼"	36 lb.	385 lb.	$279
Performance						
Challenger	17'	34"	12½"	62 lb.	650 lb.	$350
Adventurer	18'	35½"	13"	69 lb.	775 lb.	$370
Adventurer (flatwater)	18'	35½"	13-15"	70 lb.	800 lb.	$375
Scouter II (flatwater)	18'6"	32½"	11¼"	46 lb.	525 lb.	$385
Phantom	16'6"	28½"	11½"	39 lb.	450 lb.	$355
Lance	15'9"	27¼"	11½"	29 lb.	290 lb.	$340

same effort in both deep and shallow water. This canoe is not for the "average" paddler but for the advanced racer who will only settle for the best.

BLUE HOLE CANOE COMPANY
Sunbright, Tennessee 37872
Phone: (615) 628-2116

Blue Hole Canoe Company manufactures canoes and paddles from Royalex ABS sheets. The canoe hulls are single-sheet, thermo-formed with 6063 aluminum gunwales and 6061-T6 marine aluminum thwarts and seat braces, and bow and stern plates. It is interesting to note that this company is one of the few canoe manufacturers which provide grab handles as an integral part of the bow and stern plates.

Although Blue Hole canoes are very good cruising canoes on lakes and smooth rivers, they have also been designed for "fairly heavy" whitewater paddling. Hence they are very good purchases for the novice or the new paddler who plans to take courses in canoeing to learn to paddle in "wild water."

These canoes are offered with two types of seats in order to permit the purchaser to fit the boat to his type of paddling. The standard seat is a flat "kneeling" seat which is designed to enable the paddler to kneel in the boat and rest his buttocks on the front portion of the canoe seat. This seat, which is just about gunwale height, does not have any padding for long-distance comfort. The "cruising seat" is a full-width, molded, and foam-injected seat which is dropped slightly below the gunwales for better comfort over a long period of time.

The flotation used is a built-in type which is derived from the "core" of the construction materials. The manufacturer recommends that additional flotation in the form of air bags or auto inner tubes be added when heavy whitewater is being run. Such equipment would facilitate self-rescue should the boat be swamped or overturned.

Blue Hole now makes just two models—the O.C.A. Whitewater, a 16-foot model weighing 70 pounds, and the 17A Whitewater, a 17-foot model weighing 78 pounds. The authors would recommend the 17-foot model unless most of your paddling is solo, in which case the 16-foot model would probably be the better choice.

As graceful as a Thoroughbred and a seasoned jockey in the turn, the Blue Hole C.C.A. Whitewater with a skilled handler aboard sweeps through Jawbone Rapid in the Chatooga River.

Blue Hole Canoe Company

Model	Length	Width	Depth	Weight	Capacity	Approximate Price
O.C.A. Whitewater	15'9''	34''	NA	70 lb	650 lb	$465
17A Whitewater	17'3''	36''	15''	78 lb	810 lb	$495

The Blue Hole 17-A Whitewater with cruising seats takes on gear in the Okefenokee Swamp.

BOREALIS KAYAK WORKS
Box 7245
Ann Arbor, Michigan 48107
Phone: (313) 994-4064

BKW builds kayaks and canoes for white-water touring, racing, and camping. The construction and the materials used in these boats are based on their expected use. The types are as follows (the quoted material is from the BKW catalog).

Recreational Boats

"Intended for a broad range of uses, these kayaks were never meant to be the last word in either slalom or downriver racing and therefore are not the outmoded designs of previous years. Specially made for the non-specialist."

Fast Eddy (slalom K-1).

"A high-volume kayak particularly well suited for big rapids, F.E. has the speed and maneuverability of a good slalom racer. Its fine balance and performance in rough water make it a good choice" both for experts and for beginners who are learning basic white-water paddling. "Deck ridges provide knee bracing, and grab loops are recessed."

Ranger (touring K-1)

"Designed to meet the ICF regulations for downriver kayaks," the Ranger is a good, fast kayak for the novice paddler. "While the same length as a racing craft, it is broader on the waterline and has more rocker. The bow is sharp enough to make paddling on open water a pleasure," yet maneuverability and performance in whitewater are good. "In most cases the Ranger offers the greatest adaptability to a large number of users."

Dragonfly (touring K-2)

"This two-seater is uniquely designed for North American paddling. Unlike European K-2's which were intended for open water only, the Dragonfly's seating can be adjusted far enough apart to keep the bow and stern paddlers from hitting each other's blades. This is critical for running rapids, and since the open-water performance inherent in the K-2 has not been compromised, the Dragonfly . . . can both negotiate whitewater and effortlessly chew up miles of lakes."

Racing Boats

The racing-type boats have one goal: "to help the racer attain his greatest potential for winning. This means some handling characteristics will take practice to utilize properly, and the beginner should understand that these boats are more difficult to learn in."

Borealis Kayak Works

Model	Length	Width	Weight	Capacity	Price
Fast Eddy K-1	13'2"	24"	30 lb	225 lb	$295
Ranger K-1	14'9"	24"	32 lb	225 lb	$295
Otter C-1	13'2"	28"	34 lb	275 lb	$310
Blackjack K-1	13'2"	24"	22 lb	190 lb	$295
Stiletto K-1	14'9"	24"	28 lb	235 lb	$295
Dragonfly K-2	18'6"	30"	65 lb	575 lb	$425

Blackjack (slalom K-1)

"The low profile and flattened ends exploit gate-sneaking tactics. . . . Less rocker makes the boat faster, but the sharp edges near the ends improve its spinning ability in rough water."

Otter (slalom C-1)

"Excellent gate-sneaking capability although the volume is just high enough to retain good performance in big rivers. While the stern is low and sharp-edged, sections around the cockpit are fairly high-shouldered. It spins as easily as any C-1 we know of, yet is still easy to control when paddling through upstream gates."

Stiletto (downriver K-1)

"With enough volume to handle the heaviest of paddlers," this boat is designed to plane easily in shallow water. More important, this boat is designed to produce "remarkably little bottom drag in the very common river situation where planing is not quite possible. Wings are high to avoid catching the water, and this kayak turns nicely both in high brace and leaning in sweep strokes. Stability is adequate for big, turbulent rivers, though beginners will need practice to balance it."

Boat Constructions

The Standard (fiberglass-nylon-polyester)

"The Fast Eddy weighs 30 pounds when built this way. Developed with the abusive (to his boat) paddler in mind, the standard construction utilizes local reinforcement both at the bow and stern and on the deck. The foredeck can handle pop-ups and enders without collapsing, and the nylon in the bottom layup virtually ensures that the boat will never leak even under severe pounding on the rocks. Opaque gel coat prevents degradation of the structure by sunlight, and the white bottom is backed with one layer of white pigmented fiberglass so that even an old, badly worn kayak will age gracefully."

Weasel (fiberglass-nylon-polyester)

"For racers who don't wish to spend too much money. Eliminated from the standard are local reinforcement, gel coat, and one layer of fiberglass from the bottom. The resin used is stiffer, and Ethafoam walls provide internal support and flotation. Fast Eddys built this way are 24 pounds, and flotation bags (weighing 3 pounds) are not required for racing. Not the ultimate in durability, but should still last through many seasons if not abused too much."

Kevlar (PRD-49, polyester resin)

"Kevlar can be substituted for the fiberglass and nylon." The construction is similar to that of the Standard "but with one less layer in the bottom. Fast Eddy is 22 pounds this way. Kevlar has proved to be excellent for puncture resistance, but its compressive strength (important for decks!) is only slightly better than fiberglass. The weight savings it offers is worth the extra cost to many racers and to tourers who portage a lot."

CAMP-WAYS, INC.
12915 South Spring Street
Los Angeles, California 90061
Phone: (213) 532-0910

Cedar Creek's sixteen-footer shows off the grain of its Western red cedar in mirror-finish water.

Cedar Creek Canoes

Model	Length	Width	Depth	Weight	Capacity	Price
Stevie	16'	38"	12"	55 lb	NA	$850

Camp-Ways, Inc., is strictly a manufacturer of inflatable rafts and accessories. These craft are constructed of nylon-base fabric, coated with Du Pont Hypalon for body and floors. Models range from the Cormorant, a nice little 9-foot 8-inch two-person design which can be used with oars, paddle, or a four-horsepower motor, to the Havasu, the Camp-Ways top-of-the-line commercial river runner's boat, which is 17½ feet long and can be used with oars, paddles, or a motor up to ten horsepower.

In between are the Piute, a model 11 feet long; the Hopi, 12 feet; the Apache, available in 12- and 15-foot models; the Miwok, a 13½-foot two- or three-person river-running raft; the Shoshoni, a 16-foot three-person raft; and two other models that are simply referred to as "4-man deluxe boat" and "6-man boat."

Camp-Ways also offers a power sports boat called the Argonaut, available in 12-, 13-, and 16-foot models, all of which can carry four to six people. These boats come complete with windshield, rubbing strake, heavy-duty oar-

locks, inflatable pillow seat, painter, lifelines, repair kit, bellows pump, carry handles, drain plug in transom, ski rings, treated wood floorboards, carry bags for hull and floorboards, and bow D-ring.

Tube diameters range from 16½ inches on the 12-foot model to 21 inches on the 15-foot model.

CEDAR CREEK CANOES
4 Farriers Lane
Wilton, Connecticut 06897
Phone: (203) 762-0456

Cedar Creek Canoes is a new canoe builder with a small factory in Maine that hand-builds molded wood canoes. These canoes are made of laminated Western red cedar veneers, which are bonded with epoxy glue, coated both inside and outside with two coats of epoxy resin, and coated with one layer of four-ounce fiberglass cloth on the outside. At present, only a 16-foot cruiser is available. This craft is primarily for the experienced and discriminating buyer who wants a not-so-common type of boat. It is quite light and is very suitable for one person, although two people could use it for day or overnight trips.

CHESTNUT CANOE COMPANY, LTD.
PO Box 185
Oromocto, New Brunswick,
  Canada E2V 2G5
Phone: (506) 357-3338

Chestnut Canoe Company is the largest builder of canoes in Canada as well as the oldest—having been in business for more than 75 years. It also claims to be the largest canoe builder in the world. Chestnut offers fiberglass and canvas-and-wood canoes. The canvas-and-wood models are the major part of its line.

The canvas-wood canoes are constructed of cedar planking and ribs with brass fastenings over which is stretched heavy-duty seamless canvas. The canoe is next treated with a very hard coating to withstand aging and abuse, and then the entire unit is baked for approximately two weeks.

The fiberglass canoes are of hand layup using polyester resin and woven roving and mat. The bottom is reinforced with wooden

cross-ribs covered with fiberglass and with a wooden keel. Flotation is provided by a polyurethane foam enclosed in bulkheads in the bow and stern. The thwarts, gunwales, and seats are of cedar with brass fastenings.

The wood-and-canvas models range in length from the 11-foot Featherweight to the 22-foot Freight Daddy.

Chestnut offers a mind-boggling 50 models (if you can't find one to suit your needs or fancy you are in trouble), broken down into the following series: pleasure canoes, Prospector canoes, Ogilvy canoes, fiberglass pleasure canoes, cruiser canoes, Guide special canoes, Group paddling canoes, and Freight Cargo canoes.

The pleasure canoes are 11 feet through 16 feet in length. Those under 15 feet long are best suited for solo paddling, but the 15- and 16-foot models are quite capable of carrying two people and some gear for camping or fishing trips.

Says the company:

> Together with the Chestnut Freight canoes, the Prospector has played a major role in the development of the Canadian Arctic. From Gold Rush days to today, they have been in constant demand.
>
> In those early days, the only means of transportation was by water and, since portages were a necessary part of travel, a light craft that could be carried was required.
>
> Weight was a factor, but its ability to carry essential supplies for extended trips with maximum ease of mobility was a necessity.
>
> Consequently, the Prospector range of canoes were designed with greater carrying capacity per size by increasing the fullness at bow and stern, by slightly flattening the transverse section and increasing the freeboard.
>
> The bow and stern were deepened for use on rough water or in river rapids.
>
> With the introduction of the outboard motor, vee-stern models were developed for this purpose.
>
> The Prospector canoes are still used for their developed purposes, but more

A Chestnut canoe, lightly loaded, negotiates heavy whitewater.

and more are being sold for general-purpose use where a stable, steady canoe with extra capacity is required.

The Prospector canoes come in double-ended and vee-stern (similar to square stern) models, and range in length from 14 feet to 18 feet.

The 14-foot model would be very good for the solo paddler who wants to do some weekend tripping, or possibly for a hunter who wants a single canoe that can carry back the game. The 15-, 16-, 17-, and 18-foot models are more than adequate for the serious tripper who needs a canoe that can carry two people plus gear for a week or more. The 18-foot model with its 1,100-pound capacity would meet the requirements of the person who needs a canoe that can carry three or four people plus some gear.

The Ogilvy line comes in lengths of 16-, 18-, 20-, and 22-feet in the double-ended version, and in lengths of 20-feet 5-inches, 22-feet, and 26-feet in the vee-stern version.

The Ogilvy canoes are a special group that have been constructed for maximum strength, with three-inch-wide ribs spaced a half-inch apart to provide the rigid bottom required for running shoals and sandbars. These canoes were originally developed for salmon fishing in New Brunswick waters. With their wide beams, these boats offer good stability and excellent carrying capacities, and would fit neatly in to the plans of a family with one, two, or three children that likes to do a lot of canoe camping. The 26-foot vee-stern Salmo model would be best adapted for camps or for Scout groups that need a canoe that can safely carry six people and gear, even in fairly rough water.

The Freight canoes are designed for the purpose for which they are named—to haul large quantities of supplies, game, or people safely down rivers, across lakes (rough or smooth), and along coastal routes. Despite their size and carrying capacities, these canoes can be car-topped, making them a lot easier to transport than a powerboat of equal capacity. Due to their basic canoe hulls, the vee- and square-stern models can be pushed

along at speeds of 15 to 20 miles per hour with 10- to 20-horsepower motors.

The most amazing craft in the line is fittingly named the Giant. It is a 24-foot model with a 67-inch beam and a safe rough-water capacity of 7,000 pounds.

Such canoes, obviously, are not for the average paddler. They were designed for specific purposes and would best meet the needs of persons who want a boat that is reasonably portable; can be used as a fishing or cargo boat in open water; does not require a large, gasoline-guzzling motor; and—best of all—can be paddled as well as powered.

Here is a sampling of Chestnut's prices in canvas-and-wood construction, expressed in Canadian dollars:

Prospector line: Fort 16-footer, $662; Garry 17-footer, $685; Voyageur 18-footer, $708.

Ogilvy line: Henry 16-footer, $769; Jock 20-footer, $862; Trout 22-footer, $1,217.

Freight line: Hudson 17-footer, $830; Company 19-footer, $1,193; Giant 24-footer, $2,315.

CHIEF CANOES
Chief Manufacturing, Inc.
737 Clearlake Road
Cocoa, Florida 32922
Phone: (305) 636-8181

Chief Canoes are of fiberglass construction, using polyester resin and woven roving and mat for the hulls, and aluminum for the gunwales, thwarts, and seat brackets.

The company's models consist of the Brave, a 12-footer suitable for a solo paddler; the Scout, a 14-foot model suitable for one adult and gear or for two junior paddlers and gear; the 15-foot Warrior; the 16-foot Chief; the 17-foot Super Chief; and a 16-foot square-sterner. All of these models can carry two people and camping gear quite safely.

All models have foam flotation in the bow and the stern for positive buoyancy in the event of swamping or capsizing.

Kevlar reinforcement is offered on all models, at extra cost.

Chief Canoes

Model	Length	Width	Depth	Weight	Capacity	Price
Brave	12'	33"	12"	55 lb	400 lb	$169
Scout	14'	35"	12"	65 lb	575 lb	$213
Warrior	15'	36"	14"	75 lb	700 lb	$234
Chief	16'	36"	12"	75 lb	775 lb	$234
Super Chief	17'	37"	15"	95 lb	900 lb	$289
Square Stern	16'	38"	13"	85 lb	800 lb	$254

COLEMAN COMPANY, INC.
PO Box 1762
Wichita, Kansas 67201

Coleman Canoes are offered by the marine group of the Coleman Company and feature a totally new idea in canoe construction. Their hulls, seats, and end caps are constructed of molded polyethylene. The gunwales and thwarts are constructed of aluminum, as are the keelsons and the seat supports. Flotation is provided by foam in bow and stern chambers.

Heavy rapids give this solo paddler a workout in a Coleman canoe.

Coleman canoes are available in 15- and 17-foot lengths and can be purchased either assembled or unassembled. The parts are put together, according to Coleman, "much like you do with bicycles, swing sets and many other products."

These boats are a good buy for the paddler who likes to go out for a daytime cruise or even an overnighter, but are not suitable for longer trips because of their limited carrying capacity.

The company indicates that a 13-footer may be available after 1978.

Coleman Company, Inc.

	15-Foot	17-Foot
Length	15'	17'
Beam	36"	36"
Depth amidships	14"	14"
Weight	74 lb	79 lb
Maximum weight capacity	650 lb	775 lb
Suggested retail price (unassembled)	$245	$275

CORE CRAFT, INC.
Highway 2 West, Box 249
Bemidji, Minnesota 56601

Core Craft builds ten canoe models and one kayak model—all of them constructed with polyester resin and one layer of 10-ounce fiberglass cloth, one layer of mat, and one layer of 24-ounce woven roving. The keels are of redwood strips encased in fiberglass.

Decks, gunwales, thwarts, and seats are each built as a unit and bonded to the hull so as to be secure without additional fastenings. Flotation is provided by foam in generous bow and stern float chambers. In the 17-foot model this foam provides enough positive

Core Craft, Inc.

Model Length	Beam	Depth	Capacity	Weight
CTD-17	36''	13''	850 lb	78 lb
CST-17	36''	13''	850 lb	78 lb
UL-17	36''	13''	850 lb	66 lb
CWS-17	36''	13''	850 lb	78 lb
CWD-17	36''	13''	850 lb	78 lb
CST-15	35''	13''	750 lb	65 lb
UL-15	35''	13''	750 lb	54 lb
CST-16	35½''	13''	775 lb	70 lb
CSS-16	35½''	13''	785 lb	75 lb
CE-16	35½''	13''	775 lb	70 lb
Kayak 13'2''	24''	11''	300 lb	40 lb

buoyancy to carry three people when the canoe is full of water.

Core Craft canoes offer the buyer the choice of one or three keels (the latter offers better tracking characteristics than does a single keel). Most of the Core Craft models come with only one thwart or yoke, the exceptions being the CTD-17 and the CWD-17, which come with two. Weights are about average for this type of construction, although the kayak would be considered heavy by most paddlers.

Offered as optional, decorative treatments are a simulated "wood trim" on the President models and a red, white, and blue striping effect on the American.

The CSS-16 is a square-stern model for the sportsman who wants a canoe that can easily be used with a small outboard motor.

A Delhi aluminum canoe comes around a scenic bend in quiet water.

The CST-17 by Core Craft in a portage over rock.

DELHI MANUFACTURING CORPORATION
Illinois Avenue
Delhi, Louisiana 71232
Phone: (318) 878-2433

Delhi Manufacturing Corporation offers both aluminum and fiberglass canoes. See chart on next page for model specifications.

Delhi Manufacturing Corporation

Model	Width	Depth	Capacity	Price
Aluminum				
15' double-end	36½''	13''	575 lb	$284.29
17' double-end	37''	13''	720 lb	$298.57
16' square-stern	37''	13''	705 lb	$310.07
Fiberglass				
16' double-end	36½''	12½''	640 lb	$199.99

DOLPHIN PRODUCTS, INC.
PO Box 230
Wabasha, Minnesota 55981
Phone: (612) 565-3868

Dolphin builds nine models of fiberglass canoes, all of which were designed with the recreational and cruising paddler in mind. This is a nice feature because the buyer is not going to purchase a boat in which the qualities required for cruising have been compromised in order to create a boat in the racing-cruising class.

All of the Dolphin canoes are constructed of polyester resin and glass cloth, with mat and roving cloth in the hulls and Kevlar reinforcement in the sides. The gunwales and keels are made of aluminum, and the thwarts and seat frames are made of wood. Dolphin puts a generous amount of foam flotation in the ends for positive buoyancy in case of capsizing or swamping.

Being designed for cruising, these boats are quite "beamy" (the narrowest is 35 inches wide). Hence, even the 14-foot model is capable of carrying two people in quiet water. The 12-foot model, however, is more suitable for solo paddling, though it is probably adequate for two junior paddlers.

Dolphin's Princess Electric canoe is powered by a custom-made electric motor which is built into the stern and is operated by a remote-control unit near the rear thwart. With the motor removed, the rear of this canoe appears to have been caught in the jaws of some sea monster because of the notched-out area where the prop section of the motor is located. This feature should give the boat very nice paddling characteristics without the need to remove the motor.

The Dolphin line has only two drawbacks. Neither matters if you don't carry the boat far going to or from the water and if you tend to paddle on relatively protected waters. The drawbacks are the weight, and the high, wind-catching ends of two models.

Except for the 18-foot Voyager, most of the Dolphin boats are not very much heavier than boats of the same length made by other manufacturers. However, the 107-pound Voyager is heavy no matter how you look at it. It also has high, wind-catching ends which, along with the third seat, are probably the cause of the extra 20 to 25 pounds of weight.

Another model with wind-catching ends is the Chief. It is a very pretty craft, but those ends would not be at all pleasant in a cross-wind.

Dolphin Products, Inc.

Model	Length	Beam	Depth	Approximate Weight	Capacity
Dolphin Chief	17'	37''	12''	79 lb	675 lb
Voyageur	18'	38''	14''	107 lb	765 lb
Dolphin Brave	17½'	37''	12''	83 lb	685 lb
Dolphin Princess	14'	39''	12''	72 lb	635 lb
Squaw	17'	37''	12''	79 lb	675 lb
Papoose	16'	35''	12''	73 lb	590 lb
Scout	12'	35''	12''	49 lb	435 lb
Sportster					
5 hp	15'	38''	12''	90 lb	650 lb
5 hp	17'	38''	12''	107 lb	750 lb

EASY RIDER FIBERGLASS BOAT COMPANY

PO Box 88108, Tukwila Branch
Seattle, Washington 98188
Phone: (206) 228-3633

Easy Rider builds fiberglass touring and racing canoes and kayaks. Its models include two open and three decked cruising canoes, one cruising kayak, and three slalom kayaks—two C-1 and one C-2 racing designs.

These models are constructed of hand-layup polyester resin and fiberglass cloth, with a balsa inlay in the canoes for stiffness and strength. A Kevlar layup is available on special order.

The touring models start with the Scout 13, a lightweight open canoe designed for one adult or one adult and a child. This canoe has a balsa inlay, and flotation is built in under its gunwales.

The Scout 15 is similar to the Scout 13 in design and construction, but it is suitable for two people.

The TSL I is a decked touring canoe which has good touring characteristics, such as stability and comfort, while also possessing the handling characteristics of a good slalom racer. When equipped with spray skirts and propelled by experienced paddlers, this boat can go just about anywhere that a boat can go. It can also be used with a sail or an outboard motor. Its equipment includes adjustable seats, kneepads for kneeling positions, bow and stern grab loops, and painters. A front and rear cockpit and a large center cockpit make for ease in storing gear.

The TSL II is an open version of the TSL I with aluminum gunwales and thwarts and wooden seats. It is a very good boat for two people who are carrying camping gear and are paddling in fairly rough water. Its construction features include a balsa-core sandwich reinforcement in the hull. Extra-large bow and stern flotation chambers provide positive buoyancy in case of swamping or upset.

The Seawolf is a two-man decked touring canoe whose hull shape is also featured in the Beluga two-man touring kayak. The equipment of this fast canoe includes adjustable seats for sitting and kneeling positions, kneepads, bow and stern grab loops, and painters.

The Beluga is a two-place touring kayak with plenty of room under the deck for camping and other gear. Kayak blades make this boat move along considerably faster than its Seawolf version, which is designed for use with single-blade canoe paddles. Since kayaks are naturally wet boats, spray skirts are a must when you are paddling the Beluga.

The Dolphin is a single-place touring kayak which features the stability of a slalom boat and the speed of a downriver boat, thus making it a very nice cruising craft. As with all kayaks except those built of ABS plastic, float bags are recommended, though their use will reduce the space available for gear. Spray skirts are also recommended.

The Shark is a low-volume, high-performance slalom kayak for the competitor, with lots of rocker and a low profile for gate working.

The Augsburg I is a high-volume slalom competition kayak designed for people who weigh up to 180 pounds.

The Augsburg II is a high-volume competition slalom kayak designed for people who weigh from 170 to 250 pounds.

The Shoe is not really a kayak, but rather a surf-kayak. Designed expressly for surfing, it features a shovel nose that resists "pearling."

The Edge is a low-profile, low-volume slalom C-1 that has been designed for good maneuverability and for sneaking gates.

The TSL I, a decked touring canoe by Easy Rider. Note the cover on the center hatch.

Easy Rider Fiberglass Boat Company

Model	Length	Width	Depth	Weight	Capacity
Scout 13 (C)	13'	32"	12½"	40 lb	350 lb
Scout 15 (C)	15½'	34"	12½"	60 lb	600 lb
TSL I (C)	16½'	37"	14"	78 lb	900 lb
TSL II (C)	16½'	37"	13"	78 lb	900 lb
Seawolf (C)	16'8"	32"		65 lb	600 lb
Dolphin (K)	14'9"	24¼"		36 lb	300 lb
Shark (K)	13'2"	24"		32 lb	
Beluga (K)	16'8"	32"		65 lb	600 lb
Augsburg I (K)	13'2"	23¾"		32 lb	
Augsburg II (K)	13'2"	24¼"		32 lb	
Shoe (K)	9'8"	22"		35 lb	
Edge (K)	13'2"	28"		32 lb	
Sting (K)	13'2"	28"		34 lb	
Checkmate (K)	15'	31½"		48 lb	

In this table, C stands for canoe and K for kayak.

The Sting is a high-volume competition canoe which features good stability and good maneuverability. This boat is suitable for the person who is just getting into slalom racing or just wants a good, lively touring canoe.

The Checkmate is a nice, two-man slalom canoe that provides both performance and stability. The cockpits are located near the center of the boat.

EDDYLINE NORTHWEST, LTD.
8423 Mukilteo Speedway
Everett, Washington 98204
Phone: (206) 743-9252

Eddyline builds decked racing and touring whitewater canoes and kayaks. All of the Eddyline boats are vacuum-molded, glass-epoxy layups, resulting in very strong boats at low weights and good prices.

The standard Eddyline construction (used for the touring models and the racers) consists of E-glass fiberglass cloth and roving and epoxy resin. The vacuum-bagging process eliminates more excess resin than hand layup can, and it also ensures that there will not be pinholes (dry spots) in the layup.

The second construction used by Eddyline is a composite of S-glass (referred to as "superglass"), Kevlar, and epoxy resin. This construction produces incredibly strong boats which are also superlight, but because of the expense of the materials employed, these boats carry a very large price tag.

For the average cruising paddler, the standard construction is more than adequate. However, the serious competitor would do well to purchase the S-glass–Kevlar boats, which are better able to withstand the constant abuse of racing.

For the cruising paddler, Eddyline has the W-300, a ten-foot kayak designed for a child who weighs up to 110 pounds; the WTC-2, a decked touring canoe with an additional center cockpit for easy storage of gear; and the Touring C-1, a high-decked, large-volume boat that is quite suitable for day cruising or overnight trips.

The Eddyline K-1 is a medium-volume kayak that is suitable for both cruising and racing. The WSL-7 is a large-volume slalom and whitewater touring kayak that can accommodate a large paddler (solving a real problem with kayaks) and still perform very nicely in big water. The T-500 kayak has the width and the stability of a slalom boat and

Eddyline Northwest, Ltd.

Model	Length	Width	Weight	Capacity
WSL-9 (K)	13'2''	24''	27 and 21 lb	
W-300 (K)	10'		15 lb	Child to 110 lb
WTC-2 (C)	16'8''	33''	52 and 40 lb	
WSL-7 (K)	13'2''	24''	29 and 23 lb	
Touring C-1 (C)	14½'	32''	45 and 35 lb	
T-500 (K)	16'5''	25''		
WSL-C (C)				
Eddyline K-1 (K)	13'2''	24''	27 and 20 lb	
Sky Slalom C-I (C)			32 and 25 lb	

In this table, C stands for canoe and K for kayak. The heavier weight is for the "standard" model and the lighter weight for the "super" model.

The manufacturer lists the prices as: slalom — $385 in glass, $575 in Kevlar; touring — $425 in glass, $650 in Kevlar.

the length of a downriver boat. It is available with a "kick-up" rudder, a very nice feature in coastal waters or bays.

For the competitor, Eddyline offers the WSL-9, a very responsive low-volume slalom kayak; the Sky Slalom C-1; a low-volume slalom canoe; and the WSL-C, a slalom C-2 that was designed by Werner Furrer for the 1975 World Championships.

FOLBOT CORPORATION
Stark Industrial Park
Charleston, South Carolina 29405
Phone: (803) SHerwood 4-3483

The principal Folbot form is described by the manufacturer as "neither a canoe nor a kayak—and [it] must not be listed as such— rather, exclusively as the safer, saner, smarter craft." Be that as it may, for the purposes of this book and to help you, the buyer, we are going to refer to it as a kayak—because that is what it resembles and that is the way it is paddled.

Folbot boats of this type come as prefab, semirigid crafts which are built at home, much as kit boats are, or as a truly knock-down, portable-type folding kayak which can be taken apart after use and stored in two bags in a car, a closet, and so on. For cliff dwellers (people who live in high-rise apartments), this feature can be a real advantage, since it may permit you the pleasure of actually owning a boat without having to rent storage space for it.

For the do-it-yourselfer, the prefab kit has everything that is needed to build the boat except a few simple tools. The building time usually runs from 50 to 80 hours, depending upon your expertise with tools and the amount of time you have available for each work session.

Folbot offers 11 models, ranging in size from the 10-foot-long, 28-inch-wide Junior to the 17½-foot Super, which has a 37-inch beam.

These models include the Jiffy (a "heavy duty" racing model), the Glider, and the Big Glider, at 12½ feet, 14½ feet, and 16 feet, respectively. These are very beamy and stable two-person craft with enough room for some camping gear as well.

The Sporty is a very nice-looking, single-person model with a 15-foot length and a 32-inch beam. It is a good boat for the single paddler who wants the capacity of a canoe and the speed of a kayak at a reasonable weight.

The 17½-foot Super is a fine boat for a family with one or two children. It can carry two adults on the seats and one or two children on cushions in between.

The Square-Stern is a 13½-foot, 46-inch-wide powerboat model. If you are a cliff dweller who wants a power-type fishing craft, this boat deserves very serious consideration.

The Cayat, a 16-foot-long, 37-inch-wide model, is available with a 60-square-foot sailing rig.

The Sportabout is a 14-foot-long, 55-inch-wide outboard/sailboat. It is a four- to five-seater and can carry up to 100 square feet of sail (sloop rig).

GIL, INC.
1919 Hadley Road
Fort Wayne, Indiana 46804
Phone: (219) 432-3932

Gil is one of the three U.S. distributors and "service stations" for the Metzeler line of boats made in Munich, West Germany. The two others are: Inflatable Boat Center, 510 Santa Monica Boulevard, Santa Monica, California 90401, and Inflatable Boat Center, 7553 Lamar Court, Arevada, Colorado 80003.

Metzeler refers to its inflatables as "the rigid inflatables" because they take more pounds of air pressure than do comparable boats. These craft are available as rowing rafts or dinghies, powerboats, sailboats, and one- or two-person kayaks.

This is the little Joker inflatable canoe, made in West Germany by Metzeler, one of whose U.S. distributors is Gil, Inc.

The lengths of the rafts range from 7 feet 11 inches to 15 feet 6 inches, and the powerboat models range in length from 9 feet 2 inches to 14 feet 5 inches.

The one-person kayak model is 14 feet 5 inches long, and the two-person kayak models are 16 feet 9 inches and 17 feet 1 inch long. In addition, rigid (fiberglass) kayaks are offered in one- and two-person versions.

Metzeler also has three models of folding canoes. One is the Sioux S, a 15-foot 9-incher. The others are the 16-foot 5-inch Robinson 500 and the 17-foot 1-inch Seewolf.

GRANTA BOATS, LTD.
West Royalty Industrial Park
Charlottetown, Prince Edward Island,
    Canada C1E 1B0

Granta Boats, Ltd., is a British firm whose boats are distributed internationally. These boats include canoes and kayaks for touring, slalom, and surfing.

These canoes and kayaks are built either of fiberglass or of wood and polyvinylchloride (PVC) canvas. They can be purchased ready for the water or as kits. (If you don't have a place to store a canoe or a kayak, how about a knockdown one that can be stored in two or three large bags and put together in 10 or 15 minutes?)

Granta builds in and ships to all parts of the world. It has been in operation for more than 40 years, so, it seems safe to say that you might find a Granta in any country.

In fiberglass, the company offers two racing kayaks, four touring kayaks, and a 16-foot canoe. The racing kayaks are the Trophy and the Panther. The Trophy is a competition slalom kayak that is available in Super Lightweight (18–21 pounds), Lightweight (22–27 pounds), Standard (constructed of chopped mat throughout and weighing 32 pounds), and a surf version with ribs and extra buoyancy. The Panther is a slalom kayak that resembles the Trophy but has a smaller hull section and a deeper section in the rear for added stability and volume. This model is available in lightweight (22 pounds), standard (26–28 pounds), and surf-type construction.

Among the touring-class models is the Tytan, a kind of training-cruising slalom kayak which weighs about 28 pounds and comes in a deluxe version (built-in solid or translucent colors) and a standard version (one color throughout). There are also, the Wanderer, the Warrior, the Wippet, and the Wayfarer. The Wanderer is an 11-foot touring kayak. The Warrior is a 15-foot "fast touring single" (interestingly, this length of kayak is not used much in the United States for touring—due more to its "tippy" racing image than to actuality—yet is used quite extensively in Europe for this purpose). The Wippet is an attractive, large-volume "sports touring single" with a molded bucket seat, an adjustable footrest, and built-in foam flotation. It is available in either fiberglass mat or woven cloth laminate (hint: buy the woven cloth laminate). The Wayfarer is a touring double kayak, with a large, open double cockpit, two molded chair-style seats (in the deluxe model) and enough room under the forward and stern decks for some light camping gear.

Granta also builds a "rigid-touring" class of kayaks. The kayaks in this class are constructed of well-seasoned wood shaped in Swedish form and covered with a laminated PVC canvas. With the exception of the Kelo, all of these models are available in kit form. Building the kit models is generally within the capabilities of the average handyman. They are constructed by building and varnishing a wooden framework, which is then covered with a PVC canvas. The kits contain all the parts needed to construct the models, and "do it yourself" plans are available.

The rigid-touring models include the Kingfisher, which is available in a standard 14-foot model, in a 15-foot model called the Super 15, in a 17-foot model called the Kestrel; the Kiwi, an 11-foot model designed for young children; the Kelo, a 14-foot single touring kayak; and the Family K, a 20-foot kayak with seats for four persons plus a large amount of stowage space under the front and rear decks. The Granta folding kayaks are designed on the Swedish hull form and are constructed of a seasoned ash and birch framework. The hull is covered with a heavy-duty PVC-impregnated canvas, and the decks are covered with waterproof canvas. These models pack into one, two, or three bags.

The folding kayaks include the Silver Airflow, an 18-foot one- or two-person craft with inflatable buoyancy tubes and chair-type seats with separate backs; the Sprite, an 11-foot-long, single-seat touring kayak; and the Falcon, a 21-foot, four-person kayak, the sailing version of which is called the Clipper.

GREAT CANADIAN CANOE
45 Water Street
Worcester, Massachusetts 01604
Phone: (617) 755-5237

Great Canadian Canoe Company, despite its name, is a U.S. firm. Its president, John Bery, has been active in racing, designing, and building canoes for the last 20 years. Bery was among the first paddlers who "tied" makeshift covers onto their open canoes and started running heavy whitewater in those canoes on a regular basis. He later designed and built racing and cruising canoes. He also designed the first Junior canoe for paddlers weighing less than 100 pounds, thus opening up the world of canoeing to the younger paddlers.

Bery is a master boatbuilder who pays a great deal of attention to details, and thus his boats have always been in demand. About ten years ago he moved to Maine and started building boats on a full-time basis. Later he moved the company to Massachusetts.

Great Canadian builds canoes of fiberglass, aluminum, and canvas over wood and sells a line of ABS canoes manufactured by the Blue Hole Canoe Company. In addition, Great Canadian builds and sells a one-man cruising kayak that traces its lineage to an Olympic racing model which has been modified to accommodate an adult of "average" weight and size. The Great Canadian line also includes a child-sized model of this kayak, and two whitewater (closed) canoe models.

Great Canadian's fiberglass canoes range from 13 feet to 17 feet in length and from 34 inches to 37½ inches in width. They are constructed by hand-layup of 24-ounce fiberglass cloth, with 1½-ounce mat added in such areas as the keel, the bow, the stern, and the mid-

(Top) Great Canadian's 13½-footer in shallow fishing waters. (Bottom) "Wood and canvas, what a canoe should be," says the company.

paddling. It is suitable for two adults on flat cruising water or for one adult and camping gear in light whitewater.

The 16-foot 3-inch Fiberglass "Family Adventure" model was just reaching the production stage when this book was being written. It is similar to the 16-foot 2-inch Fiberglass, except that its hull is 3½ inches deeper. This permits heavier loading of people (760 pounds versus 705 pounds) and gives the craft a higher maximum load capacity (830 pounds versus 760 pounds).

The 17-foot Fiberglass "Combi" is designed for the accomplished canoeist and for the canoeist who generally uses his canoe for cruising but occasionally participates in cruising races. The boat has no keel, thus permitting faster turning, and its 23-inch-high bow permits its use in moderate whitewater. The narrow width of this boat, however, tends to make it a little less sensitive than the 16-foot 2-inch model or the 16-foot 3-inch model.

The K-1 and K-Child kayak models are of hand-layup cloth and mat construction. The K-1 is designed for cruising and racing. It is ideal for a person who weighs up to about 190 pounds and is under six feet in height. The K-Child model is a junior-sized model designed for children up to 100 pounds in weight.

The C-1 and C-2 whitewater (closed canoe) models are basically racing-type craft. Their racing characteristics make them good boats for the advanced whitewater cruising or racing paddler.

The aluminum canoes come in 15- and 17-foot lengths. These canoes are stretch-formed, with two inner-outer interlocking keels. They are constructed of heat-treated 6061 aluminum tempered to a T-6 condition, 0.051 inches thick.

The wood-and-canvas canoe is alive and doing well at Great Canadian, where it is available in 12-, 14-, 16-, and 18-foot lengths for the standard double-ended models, and in 16-, 17-, and 18-foot lengths for the square-stern models. All of these models are keelless. Great Canadian's wood-and-canvas canoes are constructed of ¼-inch-thick Canadian cedar ribs, bottom and vertical side strips with Northern ash deck, spruce gunwales, and white birch spreaders. The exterior skin is

beam. In addition, four belted-glass ribs in the midsection provide extra rigidity and strength.

The 13-foot 2-inch Fiberglass model is designed basically for use on small ponds by one or two adults weighing no more than 150 pounds each. Its short length and relatively light weight make it a nice canoe for the fisherman who often goes out alone.

The 15-foot Fiberglass model is designed for the average recreational canoeist. It will carry two adults or one adult and two children.

The 16-foot 2-inch Fiberglass model is designed for the canoeist who uses his canoe frequently, both on camping trips and for "day"

Great Canadian Canoe

Canoes

Model	Length	Beam	Depth	Weight	Maximum Load Capacity	Price
Fiberglass						
13'2''	13'2''	36''	11½''	57 lb	540 lb	$229
15'	15'0''	37¼''	12''	66 lb	640 lb	$249
16'2''	16'2''	37¼''	12½''	72 lb	760 lb	$269
"Combi"	17'0''	34''	13¼''	83 lb	800 lb	$299
"Family Adventure"	16'3''	36½''	15½''	82 lb	780 lb	$319
Aluminum						
Standard	13'	42''	13¾''	56 lb	640 lb	$319
Standard	15'	36''	13¾''	72 lb	655 lb	$319
Standard	17'	37''	13¾''	82 lb	795 lb	$329
Whitewater	15'	36''	13¾''	72 lb	655 lb	$339
Whitewater	17'	37''	13¾''	82 lb	795 lb	$349
Boats portable						
Standard—10 HP	12'1''	48''	20''	85 lb	500 lb	$299
Lightweight—10 HP	12'1''	48''	20''	76 lb	490 lb	$259
Wood/canvas with plastic						
Huron	12'	34''	12''	53 lb	510 lb	$339
Huron	14'	34''	12''	57 lb	610 lb	$379
Huron	16'	36''	12''	67 lb	770 lb	$399
Huron	18'	38''	12''	80 lb	820 lb	$439
Huron (deep)	18'	38''	14''	85 lb	860 lb	$469
Huron square stern (20'' wide)	16'	37''	14''	110 lb	780 lb	$459
Huron square stern (20'' wide)	17'	38''	14''	120 lb	820 lb	$489
Huron square stern (20'' wide)	18'	38''	14''	130 lb	860 lb	$519
Royalex® Blue Hole®						
	16'	35''	14''	72 lb	750 lb	$469 + freight
	17'2''	36''	15''	78 lb	870 lb	$479 + freight

Kayaks

Model	Length	Beam	Depth	Weight		Price
Fiberglass						
K-1	13'1½''	24''	11½''	30 lb		$259
C-1 whitewater canoe	13'2''	33''	13¼''	45 lb		$279

European touring kayak/canoe

Model	Length	Beam	Depth	Weight		Price
Fiberglass						
Can-Am	16'	29''	11½''	66 lb		$309

tightly woven canvas coated with a PVC plastic which requires "no painting." The seats are built of ash and have rawhide lacing.

Great Canadian markets a European touring kayak/canoe for use on lakes and rivers. This craft, which is quite fast, is designed to be paddled with either canoe paddles or kayak blades (the latter are preferable). Its design limits it to day cruises since there is not much room inside for camping equipment.

GREEN MOUNTAIN OUTFITTERS, INC.

Cold River Road
North Clarendon, Vermont 05759
Phone: (802) 773-3371

Keewaydin is an Indian word meaning "north west wind." When an early trader first discovered the canoe as a maneuverable form of lightweight transportation ideally suited for the rivers and lakes of North America, he borrowed the hull design known as Keewaydin for his own use. Translated into wood and canvas in the late 1800s, the Keewaydin became famous as a stable and functional craft favored by trippers and guides throughout Canada and New England.

From the Green Mountain
Outfitters brochure

Green Mountain Outfitters' Keewaydin canoes are constructed of vacuum-molded, ethylene-hexene copolymer fiberglass and Royalex. The canoes in the KT series have aluminum gunwales and thwarts and cane seats. Those in the KR and KW series have ash and mahogany gunwales, thwarts, and decks and handwoven rawhide seats.

Altogether, Green Mountain Outfitters offers seven canoe models and one kayak model.

The KT series includes the KT15, and the KT17. The KT15 is a 15-foot canoe with good beam and enough carrying capacity for one person and quite a bit of gear in rough water or for two persons and a little gear in relatively calm water. The KT17 is a 16-foot 8-inch boat with good carrying capacity for two people. At $299 it is not a bad buy for a 17-foot boat. However, it is quite heavy for its length.

In the fiberglass KR series, Keewaydin offers three models—the KR14, the KR16, and the KR18.

The KR14 is a light, stable canoe which can be handled by a fisherman, a hunter, or even a child (above age ten). The boat is light enough to be portaged by one person.

The KR16 is almost 17 feet long. This canoe is very nice for the weekend paddler and sometimes for the long-trip paddler. Its weight is about average for a canoe this size, and its hull depth is quite adequate for paddling in rough water.

The 18½-foot KR18 canoe has fast lines, good carrying capacity, and stability. It is suitable for the paddler who is looking for a good "tripping" boat. This is the original boat of the Keewaydin design.

The KW Royalex series of canoes consists of the KW16, a 16-foot model, and the KW17, which is 16 feet 10 inches in length.

The KW16 is a one- or two-person canoe that is finding great acceptance among the cruising-racing paddlers, turning up more and more frequently in their races. This was probably not the intent of its designers, but the beam, depth, and good lines of the KW16 just naturally moved it in this direction. The KW16 is a good cruising boat, quite capable of being paddled in whitewater as well as on flat lakes and rivers.

The KW17 has all the qualities of the KW16 plus enough additional carrying capacity to make it a very good boat for "tripping" with two people.

The Skat is a low-volume slalom kayak that was designed for one purpose—racing. It is available in a standard construction of fiberglass cloth and polyester resin or in a lightweight carbon fiber.

Green Mountain Outfitters, Inc.

Model	Length	Width	Depth	Weight	Capacity	Price
KT15	15'	36"	13"	60 lb	600 lb	$275
KT17	16'8"	38"	14"	77 lb	800 lb	$299
KR14	14'	36"	12"	55 lb	550 lb	$376
KR16	16'9"	36"	13"	70 lb	700 lb	$429
KR18	18½'	35"	13"	78 lb	975 lb	$487
KW16	16'	35"	14"	60 lb	600 lb	$479
KW17	16'10"	36"	15"	68 lb	800 lb	$500
Skat (kayak)	13'1"			24 or 18 lb		$353

GRUMMAN BOATS
Marathon, New York 13803
Phone: (607) 849-3211

Grumman, a name that is synonymous with aluminum canoes, builds 12 different models, each designed to do a particular task or to meet a particular problem. All of these models are constructed of stretch-formed, heat-treated, marine aluminum alloy. All fittings and seams are riveted, and neoprene sealant is used on all joints for watertightness.

Grumman canoes have three types of keels:

(1) the standard keel, (2) the bulb T-keel, and (3) the shallow-draft keel. The standard keel is a solid, T-shaped extrusion which projects downward about an inch and a half, giving the canoe good "tracking" capabilities. The bulb T-keel is used primarily on the longer 19-foot square-stern and 20-foot standard and Peace canoes to give greater strength and rigidity to the hulls. It is similar to the standard keel except for a "bulb" at the bottom. The shallow-draft keel is three-eighths of an inch deep and was designed principally for canoes that are used for whitewater paddling, where shallow draft is important, and on flat water,

A Grumman canoe with spray shirts fitted.

A flotilla of three Grummans with young paddlers moves down a serene waterway.

where the directional stability of the keel helps to maintain directional control, especially when there are side winds.

The gunwales are made of a solid aluminum-alloy extrusion and are designed to accommodate all of the company's accessories.

Flotation is provided by nonabsorbent, rigid foam at each end, enclosed inside bulkheads.

The standard double-end models come in two weight categories—standard weight and lightweight. The two categories have the same construction features except for their hulls: the standard hull is 0.050 inches thick, and the lightweight hull is 0.032 inches thick. The thinner lightweight hull dings and dents more readily than does the thicker standard hull. However, if you take trips requiring many portages or if you have a physical handicap which limits the weight that you can lift, then the lightweight model is the preferable boat. Otherwise, the best all-around model would be the standard weight.

The 13-foot double-end canoe is basically a one-man fishing model. It is not designed to carry a lot of camping equipment or to be paddled by two people in heavy water. It can, however, be used with a sailing rig (offered by Grumman as an accessory) or a motor bracket (also offered). It can be operated with a two-horsepower gasoline outboard motor or with an electric trolling motor.

Double-ended and square-sterned 15-foot models are available. Although capable of carrying two people with safety, these models are probably most suitable for the person who paddles solo more often than with a partner. The 15-footers are adaptable to just about any means of propulsion that you might want to use—whether it be paddling (single blade or double blade), poling, or sailing, or powered by a gasoline outboard motor or an electric trolling motor. The 15-foot length makes these nice boats for younger or older teenagers to learn their paddling techniques in.

The 17-foot models are also available in both a double-ended and a square-sterned version. The 17-foot double-ender is the most popular of the line and is used by schools, camps, clubs, and individuals for camping, cruising, and racing. It can be paddled by one or two persons and can carry enough camping and other gear to enable two people to cruise for up to ten days at a time. The square-stern model can be operated with a five-horsepower outboard motor without sacrificing any of its carrying capacity (as compared to the double-ended model).

The 18-foot double-ended canoe is designed primarily for families and groups that generally require a canoe that can carry three or more people. Even though this canoe is only a foot longer than the 17-footer, experience with both and conversations with many paddlers who have used both indicate that the 18-footer is far more difficult to maneuver than the 17-footer. However, the 18-footer's much greater carrying capacity could make it a better choice for a group that plans an extended cruise on a lake or a river where quick maneuvering is not required.

The 19-foot square-sterner was designed with the sportsman in mind. It can be operated with a five-horsepower outboard motor. It easily accommodates three or four people plus gear for a week's fishing or hunting trip. Its relatively light weight makes it easily "cartoppable"—a feature that some smaller "fishing" boats can't claim.

The 20-foot Peace Canoe was designed for use by large families and schools and camps. It can easily carry four to six adults or children, and its 40-inch beam makes it quite stable. It is too heavy (117 pounds) to be carried very far or over rough terrain. However, once in the water with six people paddling, it really moves right along—impressing viewers both with its speed and with the beauty of seeing those six paddles flashing together as one.

Grumman's Sportscanoe is a 15-foot 3-inch model that was designed to be paddled or to be powered by a five-horsepower motor. It is a good size for use as a fishing or hunting boat. Its oarlocks for rowing enable its occupants to sneak up on game for hunting or for photography.

Grumman Boats

Model	Weight	Width	Depth	Capacity	Price
Double-end models, standard					
13 feet	58 lb	35³/₈″	12⁷/₈″	590 lb	$340
(Lightweight same except weight 44 pounds and price $361)					
15 feet	69 lb	35¹/₈″	12¹/₈″	650 lb	$355
(Lightweight same except weight 55 pounds and price $368)					
17 feet	75 lb	36¹/₈″	13¹/₈″	755 lb	$378
(Lightweight same except weight 60 pounds and price $399)					
18 feet	85 lb	36⁵/₈″	13¹/₈″	845 lb	$400
(Lightweight same except weight 67 pounds and price $418)					
20 feet	115 lb	40¹/₈″	14″	1,110 lb	$523
20-foot Peace Canoe	117 lb	40¹/₈″	14″	1,110 lb	$578
Double-end shallow-draft keel (whitewater) models, standard					
15 feet	74 lb	35¹/₈″	12¹/₈″	650 lb	$388
17 feet	81 lb	36¹/₈″	13¹/₈″	755 lb	$411
18 feet	91 lb	36⁵/₈″	13¹/₈″	845 lb	$432
Square sterns and Sportcanoe					
15 feet	77 lb	36¹/₈″	13¹/₈″	725 lb	$400
17 feet	85 lb	36⁵/₈″	13¹/₈″	825 lb	$422
19 feet	116 lb	40¹/₈″	14″	1,100 lb	$552
15 foot 3-inch Sportcanoe	112 lb	43″	14″	440 lb	$528

HOEFGEN CANOE MANUFACTURING
SR Box 137, Highway M-35
Menominee, Michigan 49858
Phone: (906) 863-3991

Hoefgen builds fiberglass kayaks and canoes and a fiberglass duck skiff. The hulls of the canoes are constructed of hand-laid fiberglass and have an internal, fiberglass-covered wooden keelson and bottom ribs. The seats are woven cord in a hardwood frame. The gunwales and thwarts are constructed of aluminum. Flotation is provided by poured foam in the bow and the stern.

These canoes have a very interesting contour at the bow and the stern (a sponsonlike bulge) that enables them to "lift" over waves rather than drive through them.

The kayak line consists of a 13-foot 2-inch slalom kayak (ICF standard) and a 14-foot 9-inch downriver kayak (also ICF standard). These boats are of all-fiberglass construction and are quite nice, except that most competition-type kayaks being used today weigh under 30 pounds, whereas these weigh 35 and 37 pounds, respectively.

Because of its large volume, the slalom kayak would probably be a very nice cruiser. The downriver model would require some "getting used to" for the beginner. If you do most of your cruising on lakes and smooth rivers, these boats would also make "fast cruisers."

The canoes are offered in a 16-foot length with a 36-inch beam; in a 17-foot length with a 34-inch beam; and in two 18-foot models,

Hoefgen Canoe Manufacturing

Model	Length	Width	Depth	Weight	Capacity	Price
Slalom kayak	13'2"	23"	12"	35 lb		$225
Downriver kayak	14'9"	24"	12"	37 lb		$235
Duck skiff	15'	38"	14"	65 lb	600 lb	$245
Scout canoe	16'	36"	13"	70 lb	750 lb	$285
Sport canoe	17'	34"	12"	70 lb	800 lb	$295
Freighter canoe	18'	37"	13"	78 lb	1,000 lb	$310
Transport canoe	18'4"	34"	12"	75 lb	900 lb	$310

one with a 34-inch beam and one with a 37-inch beam.

The duck skiff is like an "oversized kayak." It is 15 feet long and has a 38-inch beam. It has front and rear foam flotation for safety as well as a large cockpit (2 feet by 7 feet).

LANDAU BOAT COMPANY
PO Box 750
Lebanon, Missouri 65536
Phone: (417) 532-9126

Landau Boat Company is a manufacturer of pontoon boats, bass boats, jon boats, vee-type powerboats, and canoes.

The canoes are manufactured of "work-hardened" 5052 aluminum alloy and 6061 marine alloy, heat-treated to a T-6 temper. All of the canoes are stretch-formed and riveted, with extruded keels and gunwales. The 37 Series of the Landau line features cypress thwarts and seats. There is a 16-foot square-stern model for those who wish to use a motor. Motor mounts are offered as accessories for the 15- and 17-foot models.

Two couples make camp from their Landau aluminum double-enders.

Landau Boat Company

Model	Length	Beam	Maximum Depth	Aproximate Weight	Capacity	Price
1535C	15'	36"	14"	77 lb	620 lb	$283.20
1635C	16'	36"	14"	81 lb	680 lb	$308.00
1735C	17'	36"	14"	79 lb	655 lb	$299.00
1536C	15'	36"	14"	77 lb	620 lb	$304.50
1636C	16'	36"	14"	79 lb	655 lb	$324.00
1736C	17'	36"	14"	81 lb	680 lb	$328.00
1637C	16'	37"	15"	82 lb	665 lb	$415.20
1737C	17'	37"	15"	82 lb	695 lb	$406.00

LANGFORD CANOE AND WOODWORKING, INC.

305 The West Mall, Suite 250
Etobicoke, Ontario, Canada M9C 1E7
Phone: (416) 621-8663

Langford Canoe and Woodworking, Inc., offers nine cedar-strip and canvas-covered canoes, one Royalex canoe, and eight fiberglass canoes.

The Trapper series is in cedar strip and canvas, with two-inch-wide ribs and a wooden keel. These boats are available in lengths of 12, 15, and 16 feet; 16 feet with a V-stern; 17 and 18 feet; and 19 feet with a V-stern.

The Explorer is also of cedar strip and canvas, with 1½-inch-wide ribs and a wooden keel. This 14-foot model is best suited for a solo paddler or for two paddlers on quiet water.

The Algonquin is a 16-foot canoe of cedar strip and canvas, with two-inch ribs and a wooden keel.

Langford Canoe and Woodworking, Inc.

	Price	Beam	Depth	Approximate Weight	Approximate Capacity
Trapper					
12'	$499	32"	11½"	39 lb	500 lb
15'	$540	35"	13"	62 lb	700 lb
16'	$565	36"	12½"	67 lb	800 lb
16' V-stern	$735	40"	15½"	88 lb	1,100 lb
17'	$655	35½"	13½"	76 lb	900 lb
18'	$685	37"	13"	78 lb	1,000 lb
19' V-stern	$985	47"	19"	180 lb	2,000 lb
Explorer					
14'	$505	34"	12"	53 lb	600 lb
Algonquin					
16'	$579	35½"	12½"	69 lb	800 lb
Vagabond					
16'	$535	35"	13"	75 lb	750 lb
Voyageur					
14'	$345	34"	13"	68 lb	600 lb
15'8"	$355	35"	12½"	71 lb	700 lb
16'	$365	36"	13½"	74 lb	800 lb
17'	$379	35"	14"	78 lb	900 lb
Adventurer					
14'	$319	35"	13"	62 lb	600 lb
15'8"	$329	35"	12½"	65 lb	700 lb
16'	$339	36"	13½"	70 lb	800 lb
17'	$355	35"	14"	74 lb	900 lb

Prices include U.S. duty and taxes

The Vagabond is a Royalex 16-footer with a wooden trim and no keel.

The Voyageur is a fiberglass canoe with wood-trimmed, hand-laid woven roving, a single keel, rawhide seats, and reinforcing ribs. It is available in lengths of 14 feet, 15 feet 8 inches, 16 feet, and 17 feet. The last has no keel.

The Adventurer series is made of hand-laid fiberglass with an aluminum trim. It has a single keel and reinforcing ribs, and it comes in lengths of 14 feet, 15 feet 8 inches, 16 feet, and 17 feet. The 17-foot Adventurer has no keel.

LINCOLN CANOES, INC.
Route 32
Waldoboro, Maine 04572
Phone: (207) 832-5323

Lincoln builds six models of canoes, all of which are constructed of hand-layup fiber-glass cloth and polyester resin, wooden thwarts and a wooden carrying yoke, and wood and cane seats. The gunwales are made of aluminum.

According to the company, the 16-foot Family Special is "by far our most popular model. A great family canoe, it is light, comfortable to paddle and easy to handle. The 16 is just right for fishing, float trips, or family fun. Also, available without keel for white-water use."

Of the 18-foot Cruiser Special, the company says: "With 900 pounds capacity, it will handle a good-sized family or two people and all their gear for a month. Wider and more stable, the 18 is the boat for extended trips, heavy loads, and big waters. Also available without keel for whitewater trips."

The 13-foot Two-Man Special is "just right for a father and son or daughter, a couple, or for solo paddling. It's not a boat for heavy loads or more than two people, but with a

Lincoln Canoes, Inc.

Model	Length	Width	Depth	Weight	Capacity	Price
FS16	16'	35''	13''	70 lb	600 lb	$340
CS18	18'	36''	13''	89 lb	900 lb	$398
SS14	14'	38''	13''	53 lb		$360
TS13	13'	33''	11''	59 lb	400 lb	$286
SS11	11'	33''	11''	39 lb	300 lb	$210
WS18-6	18.5'	33''	14''	80 lb		$470

Two Lincoln canoes cruise near a shoreline.

Lund American, Inc.

	Length	Beam	Depth	Capacity	Approximate Weight
Standard 17	17'	36"	13¼"	730 lb	75 lb
Lightweight 17	17'	36"	13¼"	730 lb	70 lb
CO-16	16'	36"	13¼"	710 lb	76 lb
Standard 15	15'	35½"	12¼"	650 lb	69 lb

limited load in calm waters, it's the perfect canoe—and so easy to paddle."

The 14-foot Sportsman's Special is a one-man canoe designed to provide a stable yet easy-to-handle craft for the fisherman or hunter. In protected water, this boat could be paddled by two people. Sponsons along each side for added stability and flotation are standard equipment on this little boat.

The 11-foot Single Special is a one-person craft designed for easy portaging and easy paddling.

The 18½-foot Whitewater Special is designed for cruising-class open-canoe races but is also suitable for use as a cruising-class boat for the advanced paddler.

LUND AMERICAN, INC.
PO Box 248
New York Mills, Minnesota 56567

Lund American, Inc., is principally a builder of powerboats, but it also has a small line of aluminum canoes.

The canoe line consists of a standard 17-footer, a lightweight 17-footer, a standard 15-footer, and a square-stern 16-footer. All of these models are constructed of aluminum, with extruded gunwales and keels, and all have aluminum thwarts and seats.

A. C. MACKENZIE RIVER COMPANY
PO Box 9301
Richmond Heights, Missouri 63117
Phone: (1-314) 781-7221

A. C. Mackenzie River Company specializes in the building of poling canoes and associated equipment. Its Mackenzie Poler is a 12-foot-long, 32-inch-wide, fiberglass, semiflat-bottom canoe designed for the poling canoeist. The craft has fiberglass seats which contain polystyrene foam flotation; a handmade hardwood carrying yoke; extruded aluminum gunwales; and a hull that is of hand-layup fiberglass construction. The Mackenzie Poler is available in red, white, or green. It can be used for pole cruising or competition, or as a regular cruiser with a standard canoe paddle.

MAD RIVER CANOE, INC.
PO Box 363
Waitsfield, Vermont 05673
Phone: (802) 496-2409

Mad River Canoe, Inc., builds canoes of fiberglass, Royalex, and Kevlar. All of its boats use ash for the gunwales, the thwarts, and the seat frames. The Mad River canoe is designed for rough water, and its capacity to take a beating is shown by the fact that it has won U.S. National Whitewater championships four years in a row.

This does not mean that a novice, or even an intermediate paddler, who purchases one of these boats is going to be able to go out and run big water. However, as with the automobile, the racecourse has been a good proving

A. C. Mackenzie River Company

Model	Length	Width	Depth	Weight	Capacity	Price
Mackenzie Poler	12'2"	32"	12½"	47 lb	380 lb	$265

ground for developing canoe designs and building techniques which benefit you, the recreational paddler.

For the average paddler, the fiberglass or Royalex models are more than adequate and provide good quality at a good price. The Kevlar models are designed and built for the serious racer who wants light weight and extremely strong construction to withstand the stresses of heavy whitewater competition.

Mad River canoes are from 13 feet to 18½ feet long and come in nine models that range from solo cruisers to out-and-out racing boats.

The Compatriot is a 13-foot model designed for the solo paddler. It has a V-shaped hull and is constructed of an all-cloth fiberglass layup, with ash rails and a single cane seat in the center. Tanks filled with polyurethane, in the bow and the stern, provide flotation in case of spills or swamping.

This boat is also available in a Kevlar model, which weighs about ten pounds less than the fiberglass model; however, you would have to do a lot of carrying to justify the added $230 cost.

The Missisquoi, also 13 feet long, is a square-stern model that is designed to be used with a small outboard motor. Although its length is the same as that of the Compatriot, the Missisquoi has a little more than twice the carrying capacity of the Compatriot because of its very wide beam. Like the Compatriot, it is available in fiberglass or Kevlar construction. The Kevlar model is about 12 pounds lighter than the fiberglass model. The Missisquoi has ash rails, three cane seats, a two-inch mahogany transom plate, stainless steel fasteners, and float tanks filled with polyurethane foam in the bow and the stern.

The Winooski is a stocky, deep 14-foot canoe designed for fishermen, hunters, and families. Its wide beam makes the Winooski a very stable craft for hunting and fishing, and gives the craft remarkable carrying capacity for its length. The Winooski has a V-shaped hull, ash rails and thwarts, and is available in fiberglass or Kevlar. It too has stainless steel fasteners and fore and aft float tanks filled with polyurethane.

The Explorer, a 16-foot model, is available

A Mad River canoe speeds through the foam.

The Winooski moving under sail.

in Royalex or Kevlar construction. With its 15-inch depth at the center and its 22-inch-high bow and stern, the Explorer is a good boat for paddling on lakes and rivers where large waves may be encountered. The hull is V-shaped with a good rocker at both ends for easy maneuvering.

The Kevlar Explorer is designed principally for the "long tripper" who wants or needs a boat that can take a great deal of punishment and keep on going. Both the Kevlar model and the Royalex model have ash rails and thwarts and cane seats. The Kevlar model has foam-filled float tanks in the bow and the stern. The Royalex model contains a

unicellular foam core which generates the flotation as an integral part of the hull.

The Screamer is a 16-foot 3-inch model designed for use as a singles-class racing craft. It has been designed strictly as a racing boat, and it is not recommended for the inexperienced paddler. It is available in both fiberglass and Kevlar, and in this case the purchaser would do well to spend the extra money for the Kevlar model. Its standard features include the V-shaped hull, the ash rails and ash center thwart, the internal keel, stainless steel fasteners, and flotation tanks in the bow and the stern that are filled with polyurethane foam.

Mad River Canoe, Inc.

Model	Length	Width	Depth	Weight	Price
Royalex Explorer	16'	35''	15''	70 lb	$495 in Royalex; $769
Kevlar Explorer	16½'	35''	15''	55 lb	in Kevlar 49
Malecite	16½'	33''	13''	62 lb in fiberglass; 45 lb in Kevlar	$429 in fiberglass; $715 in Kevlar 49
T-W Special	18½'	32''	14½''	80 lb in fiberglass; 65 lb in Kevlar	$579 in fiberglass; $869 in Kevlar 49
Endurall	16'	32''	13''	65 lb	$495 in Royalex
Winooski	14'	39''	15''	60 lb in fiberglass; 45 lb in Kevlar	$399 in fiberglass; $699 in Kevlar 49
Missisquoi (square stern)	13'	39''	15''	75 lb in fiberglass; 63 lb in Kevlar	$495 in fiberglass; $759 in Kevlar 49
Compatriot	13'	30''	12''	40 lb in fiberglass; 30 lb in Kevlar	$345 in fiberglass; $575 in Kevlar 49
Screamer	16'3''	27''	15''	60 lb in fiberglass; 48 lb in Kevlar	$419 in fiberglass; $699 in Kevlar 49

The 16-foot Endurall was the first Royalex canoe built by Mad River. It has a flat bottom with a good rocker, making it a very stable and maneuverable canoe (a major factor in its popularity for open-canoe slalom racing). It has a Royalex hull with built-in flotation; ash rails, thwarts, and seat frames, and stainless steel fasteners.

The Malecite is a 16-foot 6-inch fiberglass model that has been designed for the canoeist who wants speed, maneuverability, and good carrying capacity in a single package.

MARAVIA CORPORATION
857 Thornton Street
San Leandro, California 94577
Phone: (415) 483-2820

Maravia is a builder of inflatables. Its line of dinghies supplements its well-known boats for use on whitewater rivers. These dinghies include the Ultra-Lite Breeze. Built of Kevlar 29, it can carry four persons; weighs less than 20 pounds exclusive of oars; and fits on a standard pack frame leaving room for other gear as well.

Says the company:

Maravia Corporation offers the professional whitewater outfitter or the experienced amateur the ultimate in inflatable riverboat design, construction and durability.

All Maravia boats are designed and manufactured in the United States. Detailed consideration has been given to those characteristics most desired by the professional: ruggedness and durability, maneuverability, light weight and ease of maintenance. All designs include those requirements anticipated in forthcoming U.S. Coast Guard regulations.

The coated fabrics used in the construction of the boats were selected following extensive research. . . . They [have excellent)] strength and resistance to abrasion, hydrolytic action and fungicidal growth. Their ability to withstand temperature fluctuations, long-term exposure to ultra-violet rays and ozone are excellent.

The construction methods utilized by Maravia incorporate patented and proprietary techniques, resulting in a boat main frame, regardless of size, which has a total of three seams only. The boats are constructed using a combination of advanced adhesive technology and dielectric welding.

The following features are listed as standard:

- Stainless-steel D-rings.
- Self-bailing floors on all boats of over 18 feet in length.
- Laced-in thwart tubes.
- Minimum of six separate air compartments.
- Recessed urethane valves with air-check feature.
- Three-eighths-inch nylon-braid life line.

Maravia lists the following features as options:
- Air-tight zippers in thwart tubes, providing dry storage.
- Variable bow and stern lifts.
- Variable lengths.
- Extra thwart tubes.

MICHI-CRAFT CORPORATION
19 Mile Road at 200th Avenue
Big Rapids, Michigan 49307
Phone: (616) 796-2675

Canoes built by Michi-Craft Corporation are constructed of stretch-formed, heat-treated 6061T4 marine aluminum alloy or standard 5052H888 marine aluminum alloy. In either case, the aluminum is 0.050 inches thick. All of these canoes feature extruded aluminum stems, keels, thwarts, gunwales, and ribs, and all have molded, polystyrene foam flotation in the bow and the stern for positive flotation in case of swamping or spills. The company also offers the buyer a choice in rivets—that is, flush or roundhead. In either case, the rivet diameter is 5/32 inches.

The seats are constructed of 0.063-inch-thick aluminum and are permanently painted to prevent the aluminum oxide from rubbing

A sixteen-foot square-sterner by Michi-Craft operating under power.

off on the paddler's clothing and skin. In addition, the entire interior is finished with a nonskid gray paint which helps to reduce reflected glare and eye fatigue.

Michi-Craft canoes come in lengths of 12, 13, 15, 16, and 17 feet and in double-ended and square-stern models. In addition, the buyer has the choice of standard weight heat-treated, lightweight heat-treated, and standard weight non-heat-treated models and of a whitewater model which is heat-treated and features a "flat" keel. Michi-Craft canoes also feature a "safety foil," which is a longitudinal widening of the hull just above the waterline (similar to a sponson). The safety foil tends to give Michi-Craft models additional stability over "smooth-sided" models.

The square-stern canoes come in 12-, 14-, and 16-foot lengths and will handle motors of up to five horsepower. The 12-foot model has a beam 44 inches wide, which makes it a nice fishing or hunting craft for one person.

The 12-, 13-, and 14-foot canoes are basically one-person craft. The 15-foot model can carry two people and some gear. However, the 16- and 17-foot models would be preferable for the serious tripper-paddler.

Michi-Craft Corporation

	Double-End Canoes					Square-Stern Canoes				
	T-15	S-15	F-15	W-15	T-16	S-16	F-16	T-14	S-14	L-12
Type of Aluminum	Heat-Treated	Standard	Heat-Treated	Heat-Treated	Heat-Treated	Standard	Heat-Treated	Heat-Treated	Standard	Heat-Treated
Length	15'	15'	15'	15'	16'	16'	16'	13'10''	13'10''	11'9''
Width	37''	37''	37''	37''	36''	36''	36''	37''	37''	44''
Depth	13''	13''	13''	13''	13''	13''	13''	13''	13''	12''
Weight (lb)	69	69	69	70	75	75	75	74	74	54
Capacity (lb)	660	660	660	660	795	795	795	715	715	700
Price	$353	$334	$369	$385	$399	$379	$429	$379	$359	$359

	Double-End Canoes					Lightweight Canoes		13-Foot Canoes
	T-17	S-17	F-17	W-17	L-15	L-17	L-13
Type of Aluminum	Heat-Treated	Standard	Heat-Treated	Heat-Treated	Heat-Treated	Heat-Treated	Heat-Treated
Length	17'	17'	17'	17'	15'	17'	13'
Width	36''	36''	36''	36''	37''	36''	44''
Depth	13''	13''	13''	13''	13''	13''	12''
Weight (lb)	78	78	78	79	54	62	49
Capacity (lb)	780	780	780	780	665	790	690
Price	$377	$359	$399	$410	$359	$389	$339

MID-CANADA FIBERGLASS, LTD.
Box 1599
New Liskeard, Ontario, Canada P0J 1P0
Phone: (705) 647-6549

Scott Canoes, manufactured by Mid-Canada Fiberglass, Ltd., are constructed of fiberglass-reinforced plastic (polyester resin and mat and cloth layup), with extruded aluminum gunwales, cast aluminum end caps, and extruded aluminum thwarts and seat frames. Also available are Ethafoam sponsons for added stability.

Flotation cells in the bow and the stern provide positive buoyancy in the event of upset or swamping.

Models include a 12-foot Feather canoe with sponsons; a 14-foot paddling canoe; a 15-foot paddling canoe; a 17-foot paddling canoe; a 14-foot V-stern canoe for use with an outboard motor; and 16- and 18-foot freighter canoes, both with V-sterns for use with outboard motors.

All models are available in Kevlar.

MOHAWK MANUFACTURING COMPANY
PO Box 668
Longwood, Florida 32750
Phone: (305) 834-3233

Mohawk offers eight models of fiberglass canoes.

The Guide models are constructed of fiberglass-reinforced plastic (mat and woven roving), with extruded aluminum gunwales, aluminum end caps and ribs, and aluminum seat frames with canvas seats. They come in lengths of 14, 16, and 17½ feet.

The Ranger is a 17-footer with a rounder bottom than the Guide models. This makes the Ranger faster and easier to paddle, but it also means that more skill is required to handle the Ranger through turns.

The 15-foot 11-inch Lancer is wide and flat-bottomed, with a wide shoe keel, making it suitable for shallow or rocky rivers.

The Square Stern has the same length and

Mid-Canada Fiberglass, Ltd.

Model	Length	Width	Weight	Capacity	Price (in Canadian Funds)
Feather	12'	44"	45 lb	658 lb	$274
Paddling	14'	35"	55 lb	572 lb	$262
Paddling	15'	36"	65 lb	796 lb	$298
Paddling	17'	38"	85 lb	950 lb	$322
"Y" stern	14'	38"	85 lb	897 lb	$322
"Y" stern	16'	42"	100 lb	1,095 lb	$349
Freighter "McKenzie"	18'	46"	150 lb	1,300 lb	$499
Freighter "James Bay" "Y" stern	22'6"	45"	450 lb	—	—
Whitewater	15'	36"	65 lb	796 lb	$298
Whitewater*	15'	36"	50 lb	—	$499
Paddling*	15'	36"	50 lb	—	$499

*Kevlar

beam width as the Lancer. It will take outboard motors of up to three horsepower.

The Pack is only 10½ feet long and weighs only 30 pounds. It is easily paddled by children.

The Whitewater River is a 16-footer with the same construction as the Guide models, except that it has more flotation, longer decks, and a higher freeboard, plus more rocker in the bow and the stern for greater maneuverability.

The ABS Royalex Whitewater model is, as its name indicates, constructed of ABS Royalex, a Uniroyal laminate of acrylonitrite butadiene styrene, with heat-treated aluminum gunwales, and aluminum thwarts and seat supports. The seats are made of fiberglass. The thwarts are attached with self-locking nuts; thus, they can easily be removed and additional foam flotation blocks installed when the boat is going to be used in heavy whitewater.

The Jensens are a line of racing and high-performance canoes that were designed by Eugene Jensen. These boats are basically for use by advanced canoeists, and despite the

Mohawk Manufacturing Company

Model	Length	Width	Weight	Price
Guide	14'	35"	60 lb	$229.00
Guide	16'	35½"	72 lb	$240.00
Guide	17½'	36"	82 lb	$259.00
Ranger	17'	34"	67 lb	$240.00
Lancer	15'11"	36"	75 lb	$240.00
Square Stern	15'11"	36"	85 lb	$275.00
Pack	10½'	27"	30 lb	$99.50
Whitewater River	16'	35½"	80 lb	$259.00
ABS Royalex Whitewater	16'	34"	75 lb	$420.00
Jensen (Cl)	16'	28"	40 lb	$299.00
Jensen (S)	16'	34"	55 lb	$299.00
Jensen (S)	18'	33"	58 lb	$299.00
Jensen (FW)	18½'	32"	45 lb	$350.00
Jensen (WW)	18½'	34"	55 lb	$350.00

Heavy whitewater keeps paddlers
busy in a seventeen-footer by MonArk.

designer's claims to the contrary, they are
mainly suitable for use in racing or by racers
(active and retired) who still want the feel of
a racing hull. The construction of the Jensens is similar to that of the Guide models, except that some refinements have been made
to meet the requirements for racing craft. If
you think that you would like a boat of this
type, try one out first. They require some
"getting used to."

MonArk BOAT COMPANY
PO Box 210
Monticello, Arkansas 71655
Phone: (501) 367-5361

Three lengths of aluminum canoes are offered by MonArk boats—15, 16, and 17 feet.
The 16-footer is a square-sterner designed to
be used with outboard motors of up to 5
horsepower.

The three models are constructed of
stretch-formed and heat-treated aluminum,
0.050 inches thick, with extruded keels and
gunwales. The thwarts and seats are made of
aluminum tube. All three models have aluminum ribs in the bottom and can be purchased with either a standard or a whitewater
keel.

MORLEY CEDAR CANOES
PO Box 147
Swan Lake, Montana 59911

For those of you who want a really beautiful
and quality-built canoe, round up about
$800 and send it to Greg Morley of Morley
Cedar Canoes and then be prepared to wait a
few months to receive your canoe. Is a canoe
worth that? Yes, if you want a handcrafted
canoe of Western red cedar strips, with oak
gunwales, thwarts, and seats, and with a finish of fiberglass cloth and epoxy.

A Morley canoe looks as if you should put
it up over the mantelpiece, but actually it is
designed to be paddled in heavy whitewater
and to be bounced off rocks and snags and
go home looking just as pretty as when you
started.

Morley offers seven models : the Guide, in
lengths of 15, 16, 17, and 18 feet; 14- and
16-foot square-sterners; and a beautiful little
single-hander called the Lightweight. Morley
will also modify any of its designs to give you
the exact canoe you are looking for.

Remember, these boats are not for the
paddler who just wants a canoe; they are for
the discriminating paddler who wants the
very best and is willing to pay for it.

NATURAL DESIGNS
2223 North 60th Street
Seattle, Washington 98103
Phone: (206) 525-0109

MonArk Boat Company

Model	Length	Width	Depth	Weight	Capacity	Price
4020	15'	35½"	13"	68 lb	555 lb	$329.23
4024	16'	36"	13"	80 lb	655 lb	$353.85
4026	17'	36"	13"	78 lb	675 lb	$345.85

Morley Cedar Canoes

Model	Length	Width	Weight	Capacity	Price
Guide	15'	35''	70 lb	750 lb	$775
Guide	16'	35''	78 lb	800 lb	$785
Guide	17'	36''	85 lb	900 lb	$800
Guide	18'	36''	90 lb	1,000 lb	$825
Square Stern	14'	35''	75 lb	750 lb	$815
Square Stern	16'	36''	105 lb	850 lb	$840
Lightweight	13'	32''	40 lb	500 lb	$735

Natural Designs offers racing and cruising canoes in fiberglass, Kevlar, S-glass, and nylon-reinforced plastic. Its models have adjustable seats and foam walls. At this writing, no other information was available. You should request a catalog and pictures in order to determine what the company has to offer.

NOAH COMPANY
Star Route Box 68
Bryson City, North Carolina 28713
Phone: (704) 321-4529

Noah offers both cruising and hot racing designs in K-1's, C-1's, and C-2's. Kevlar and vinyl ester resin are used as standard construction for all of the company's models. This yields very strong and lightweight boats. (Fiberglass is offered as an option.)

Noah's racing K-1, called the Triton, is claimed to be "one of the smallest volume boats ever built." It is designed for one purpose: to negotiate a slalom course quickly and to "sneak" as many gates as possible.

Although Noah claims great feats of river running as examples of the K-1's suitability for cruising, this boat is for the advanced and expert paddler. Noah is coming out with a cruising/racing model in 1978, which, if it is like the company's C-1's, would be more suitable for river running.

The JaPe C-1 comes in three models: the Atlantis, a very nice decked C-1 with a racing heritage and with a little extra volume for comfort and for carrying some gear; the Universal, a racing/cruising design of smaller volume; and the Tritonia, an out-and-out

racing C-1 with a low volume similar to that of the Triton K-1.

The decked C-2, called the Moldau, is referred to as a racing/cruising C-2. This boat is for the runner of heavy rivers who wants a little bit of volume and good maneuverability.

Noah also offers the Tritonia C-2, a new racing design which is still being tested.

Some of the Noah boats are available in three degrees of completion, with ascending prices: as seamed kits, partly finished, and finished.

NONA BOATS, INC.
977 West 19th Street
Costa Mesa, California 92627
Phone: (714) 548-1010

Nona manufactures seven models of canoes and two models of kayaks. All of its boats are constructed of fiberglass and polyester resin, and all have one-piece decks which include end caps. Nonskid seats and thwarts and rolled gunwales are featured on the canoes.

All of the canoes except the 15-foot California '49er are keelless, as are all the kayaks. All Nona models have flotation chambers fore and aft for positive buoyancy.

The Nona canoe models are:

The 10½-foot Shadow, a Rushton-style canoe designed for single-handed paddling.

The 15-foot California '49er, designed for one or two people.

The 18½-foot Catalina whitewater cargo canoe, a family-type canoe with a safe carrying capacity of approximately 1,100 pounds.

Nona Boats, Inc.

Canoe Models	Length	Width	Weight	Capacity	Price
Shadow	10'6''	27''	23 lb	325 lb	$215
California '49er	15'4''	34''	60 lb	625 lb	$360
Catalina	18'6''	37''	90 lb	1,100 lb	$469
Poseidon	17'	36''	75 lb	950 lb	$415
Deck Canoe—					
3-Hole	17'	36''	95 lb	950 lb	$496
Enterprise	25'	45''	220 lb	2,200 lb	$1,250
Kayaks					
K-1 Slalom, Standard	13'3''	23''	35 lb	325 lb	$285
K-1 Slalom, Deluxe	13'3''	23''	35 lb	375 lb	$314
K-1 Tourer, Standard	13'3''	23''	35 lb	325 lb	$285
K-1 Tourer, Deluxe	13'3''	23''	35 lb	325 lb	$314
K-1 Slalom—					
Tourer, Standard	13'3''	25''	35 lb	325 lb	$285
K-1 Slalom—					
Tourer, Deluxe	13'3''	25''	35 lb	325 lb	$314

The War Canoe, a 25-footer capable of carrying up to a ton.

The 17-foot Poseidon, an all-around boat for cruising.

The 17-foot Deck Canoe, which is similar to the Poseidon, except that it has a fiberglass deck with three hatches and contoured, tractor-type seats mounted on pedestals.

The Nona kayak models consist of the 13-foot 3-inch Scamp K-1 touring kayak and the 13-foot 3-inch K-1 Slalom-Tourer, a combination slalom racing/touring boat with cockpit that is a little larger than that of the Scamp.

NORCAL FABRICATORS, INC.
PO Box 250
Callander, Ontario, Canada P0H 1H0
Phone: (705) 752-1211

Norcal Fabricator's Radisson is a rather unusual aluminum canoe. Its one-piece hull is constructed of 5052 marine aluminum. This is primed with a zinc chromate epoxy undercoating; the finish coat colors are either "barktone" or "forest green."

On the inside, the Radisson has extruded aluminum ribs (about 16 to 18) and a foam liner from the bow to the stern, making the canoe quiet and practically unsinkable. The end caps are made of nylon, as are the carrying handles at the bow and the stern. In addition, detachable foam sponsons set near the waterline act as both stabilizers and bumpers.

The Radisson models come in two lengths, 12 feet and 14 feet, and each model is offered in both double-pointed and square-sterned versions. These boats were designed for fishermen and hunters. Their light weight makes for easy portaging. They are basically one-person canoes, though the 14-foot models could carry two persons in relatively calm water.

Norcal Fabricators, Inc.

Model	Length	Width	Depth	Approximate Weight	Capacity
12' Pointed	11'6''	36''	13''	34 lb	600 lb
12' Square Stern	11'6''	36''	13''	37 lb	600 lb
14' Pointed	13'6''	36''	13''	41 lb	850 lb
14' Square Stern	13'6''	36''	13''	44 lb	850 lb

Northeast Canoe Manufacturing

Model	Length	Width	Weight	Capacity	Price
Newporter	12'	31''	35 lb	300 lb	$264
Fisherman	13'4''	33''	43 lb	400 lb	$313
Clyde River	14'	32''	45 lb	400 lb	$292
Northeaster	16'4''	33''	68 lb	900 lb	$340
Adventurer	16'3''	33''	65 lb	900 lb	$370
Cruiser	18'5''	33''	75 lb	1,100 lb	$470
Racing Models					
SL I	13'4''	31''	40 lb	NA	$300
D.E.	16'4''	28''	50 lb	NA	$361
F.W. Challenger	18'5''	32''	60 lb	NA	$408
D.R. Challenger	18'5''	32''	75 lb	NA	$470
Cruiser	18'5''	33''	78 lb	NA	$470

NORTHEAST CANOE MANUFACTURING

248 Indian Point Street
Newport, Vermont 05855
Phone: (802) 334-2627

Northeast Canoe Manufacturing builds recreational, sport, and racing-type open canoes. The recreational and sport models are generally constructed of hand-layup fiberglass reinforced with polyester resin, and the racing models are generally constructed of fiberglass or carbon fiber.

The sport models are the 12-foot Newporter, a nice lightweight canoe which is suitable for one person on a quiet lake or stream, and the 13-foot 4-inch Fisherman, a good little boat which is also pretty much limited to one person but can handle a little rougher water because of its greater length.

Northeast offers a 14-foot model that is suitable for the solo recreational paddler and a 16-foot 4-inch model that meets the needs of the recreational paddler who likes company plus lunch and dinner and maybe a tent for overnight trips.

The cruiser was built for the serious recreational paddler who uses his boat for extended trips or needs a craft that can safely carry a passenger as well as another paddler (and handle a bit of rough water). Its 18-foot 5-inch length and its 1,100-pound carrying capacity offer the owner many options.

For the competitor, Northeast offers slalom and downriver models that are reinforced with carbon fiber for added stiffness and strength. These boats range in length from 13-feet 4-inches for the slalom model to 18-feet 5-inches for the downriver Challenger model. In addition, there is the 18-foot 5-inch Cruiser model, which was designed for the cruising-class races.

All of the Northeast boats come with aluminum rails (ash is available), ash thwarts and seat frames, and rawhide seats.

The rawhide seats and rear flotation chamber of a Northeast canoe show up well here, as do the boat's lines.

OLD TOWN CANOE COMPANY
Old Town, Maine 04468
Phone: (207) 827-5513

Old Town Canoe Company, a name that is synonymous with the wood-and-canvas canoe, is the oldest canoe manufacturer in the United States. Old Town doesn't just *build* these canoes—it literally *handcrafts* them.

Each Old Town canoe—with its extra half-ribs, rub rails, full-length stem band, and floor rack—has the unique quality of becoming an instant heirloom. If you don't think these boats will last, go poking around some of the older canoe clubs in your area—the chances are that you will run into at least one Old Town canoe that is around 50 years old. So if you want the best available and you have the money (these canoes are not cheap!), place your order with Old Town, and in a couple of months you will have something of real pride and joy.

Old Town also builds in fiberglass and in a special ABS material called Oltonar. Boats built in these materials are as carefully crafted as boats built in wood and canvas, with extra attention paid to such details as stiffness, strength, weight, and fittings.

The Old Town canoe and kayak line reflects the diverse needs of the paddlers whom Old Town serves. For example, the ICF whitewater boats reflect Old Town's efforts to give the U.S. whitewater teams the best equipment available when those teams represented their country in world championship competitions.

The ABS Oltonar canoes come in a wide choice of models, from the Chipewyan 12 lightweight Pack canoe to the deep-hull Chipewyan 18. In between are the Chipewyan 14, which is primarily a fishing and recreational craft for one or two people; the Chipewyan 15, a nice two-man craft for small lakes and rivers; the Chipewyan 16, a very nice recreational boat which can be used in most types of water with good maneuverability and stability; and the Chipewyan 17, the major craft of the line, which is designed for use on long-distance expeditions but is also excellent for family-type use.

Also available in Oltonar are the Rockport, a rowing dinghy which can be used with an outboard motor of up to 7½ horsepower; the Rangeley, a double-ended 16-foot rowing canoe with two rowing seats, carlocks, and chains (a good boat for fishermen who don't or won't use outboard motors); and the Snapper, an ICF-class slalom kayak that is just as much at home when performing "cruising" duties as it is when racing.

In fiberglass, Old Town offers the paddler 14 models of canoes and four kayak models. These include such specialty craft as the Rushton, the Surfer, the Slalom, the Tourer, the Sockeye, the Wenatchee, and the Berrigan.

The Rushton, a 10-foot-long, 27-inch-wide canoe, weighs only 19 pounds and is designed to be packed in by, and used by, one person. The Surfer, a kayak that has been specially designed for surfing, comes complete with a molded seat, form knee braces, five-position foot brace, and a stern grab loop. The Slalom is an ICF-class competition kayak. The Tourer is an ICF-class downriver racing kayak which also makes a good cruising kayak for flat or moderately rough lakes and rivers. The Sockeye is a two-person cruising kayak with a foot-controlled "knock-up" rudder and foam seats and backrests. The Wenatchee is a C-1 competition canoe which meets ICF rules. (It also makes an excellent cruising boat for the solo paddler who wants to do a bit of whitewater paddling.) The Berrigan is a two-man, decked whitewater canoe with a third cockpit for cargo. This boat is designed to meet the ICF rules for two-man slalom canoes, but it is very comfortable for long-distance cruising.

The Carleton and Casco lines are standard-type fiberglass canoes.

The Carleton 14, 16, 17, and 18 are of much the same design as the Chipewyan. However, the bows and sterns have been made a lot sharper because sharper curves can be molded in fiberglass than in ABS. There are also two 17-foot square-stern models in the Carleton line. One of these models is a regular square-sterner; the other has molded-in sponson flotation pads along the entire length of the gunwales from the foredeck to the rear deck.

The Casco line consists of the 16-foot Traveler and the 18-foot Fisher. These boats are very similar to the Carleton 14, 16, and 18. However, the gunwales, seats, and decks are molded as one piece, and there are no thwarts between the seats—thus offering a little more room for people or cargo.

Another Old Town fiberglass model is the Wahoo, a sailing canoe with slots in the hull for the dagger boards, an aluminum mast, a tilt rudder with a steering tiller, and a 75-square-foot sail. The Wahoo's construction is similar to that of the Traveler except for the dagger-board slots.

Old Town also offers the Laker, which the company calls an "inexpensive canoe designed for relaxing, quiet-water paddling. This new 16-foot craft is perfect for sportsmen and for families who enjoy leisure canoeing on small lakes, ponds, and other flat waters.

"Although of rugged, bonded-fiberglass construction," adds the company, "Laker is not recommended by Old Town for white- or wild-water use. Nevertheless, Laker provides ample margins of capacity, serviceability, and safety when used for general recreation in quiet waters."

The wood-and-canvas canoes for which Old Town is famous come in four basic lines—the Guide series, the OTCA series, the Trapper, and the Molitor.

The Guide series is perhaps the most familiar and popular of the Old Town canoes. The canoes in this series come in lengths of 16, 18, and 20 feet. With their long, flat floors, these canoes can carry a large amount of cargo yet have a very shallow draft.

The canoes in the OTCA series come in lengths of 16, 17, and 18 feet. These models are noted for their high bows. They are considerably lighter than the Guide models of the same lengths.

The Trapper is a 15-foot model which is available with a canvas covering or in a clear,

natural finish. At 55 pounds, the Trapper is easy to portage, making it a nice canoe for two people who have to do some portaging along the way to their favorite fishing or camping spot.

The Molitor is a sleek-looking 17-footer with long decks and a stem line that curls back about 2 to 2½ feet from the bow. This model has no thwarts other than the seat brackets, but it can be rigged for sailing should the desire arise.

Old though it is, Old Town is never at a loss for new twists in using canoes. Under the heading "Canoeski," it recently described how to "canoggan"—that is, use a canoe for a fast charge down a ski slope. Said the company:

Skiing on Alpine slopes may be the ultimate in winter sports, but you never know. For instance, canogganing is as fresh and exciting as a breath of cold winter air.

A hair-raising dash down the snow-covered side of a mountain by canoe is what canogganing is all about. As with any new sport, it should be approached obliquely rather than head-on. We suggest several trial runs on lesser slopes before attempting the "big one."

Controlling direction once under way is achieved by paddles, brooms, or ski poles used discreetly while heeling the craft to port or starboard with body English. All of this is occurring as you careen down the slopes at speeds which may range from 35 to as high as 50 miles per hour, depending on the quality of the snow and the angle of incline. For this reason it is sound canogganing practice to scout your intended path of trajectory for sharp rock projections or other hazards before uttering the traditional blood-chilling alarm which warns the countryside that another canogganing run is about to begin.

If you do not live near a ski slope, a variation of the foregoing ride may be achieved by towing your canoe or kayak behind a skimobile.

Old Town Canoe Company

Oltonar canoes

Model	Length	Width	Depth	Weight	Price
Ranger	17'2''	37''	15''	79 lb	$780
Rangeley	16'	44''	14''	90 lb	$775
Chipewyan line					
Pack	11'11''	32''	12½''	40 lb	$475
Hunter	14'	35''	12''	53 lb	$505
Pathfinder	14'10''	36''	13½''	64 lb	$535
Camper	16'	36''	12''	69 lb	$545
Tripper	17'2''	37''	15''	77 lb	$575
Voyageur	18'	37½''	13½''	79 lb	$595

Fiberglass canoes

Model	Length	Width	Depth	Weight	Price
Laker-16	16'	36''	12''	72 lb	$375
Laker-18	18'	37½''	12''	85 lb	$415
Rushton	10½'	27''	10''	19 lb	$365
Carleton line					
Sport	14'	35''	12''	72 lb	$460
Adventurer	16'	36''	12''	81 lb	$480
Explorer	18'	37½''	12''	93 lb	$530
Square End	17'	37½''	11¼''	99 lb	$590
Sponson	17'	42''	13''	116 lb	$740
Casco line					
Traveler	16'	36''	12''	85 lb	$640
Fisher	18'	37''	12''	99 lb	$680

Wood canoes

Model	Length	Width	Depth	Weight	Price
Guide-16	16'	35''	12''	68 lb	$1,035
Guide-18	18'	37''	12''	83 lb	$1,075
Guide-20	20'	39''	13¼''	97 lb	$1,195
OTCA-16	16'	36''	12''	67 lb	$1,045
OTCA-17	17'	35''	12''	72 lb	$1,065
OTCA-18	18'	37''	12''	77 lb	$1,085
Trapper	15'	35½''	11½''	55 lb	$1,025
Molitor	17'	35''	12''	79 lb	$1,265

Covered craft (kayaks and decked canoes in fiberglass or Oltonar)

Model	Length	Width	Depth	Weight	Price
Surfer (K)	10½'	24''	12''	32 lb	$450
Slalom (K)	13'1½''	24''	11¾''	31½ lb	$460
Tourer (K)	14'8''	24½''	12''	35 lb	$470
Sockeye (K)	16'5''	31½''	15¼''	65 lb	$695
Snapper (K)	13'1½''	24''	13''	37 lb	$595
Wenatchee (C)	13'2''	28''	12½''	42 lb	$645
Berrigan (C)	16'	33½''	14''	65 lb	$775

Osagian Boats, Inc.

Model	Length	Beam	Depth	Weight	Capacity	Price
15' Standard*	15'	36''	14''	70 lb	690 lb	$320
16' Square Stern*	16'	36''	14''	80 lb	700 lb	$360
17' Standard*	17'	36''	14''	80 lb	780 lb	$340
17' Whitewater	17'	36''	14''	80 lb	780 lb	$360

*Optional—inner extrusion T-Cap keel.

OSAGIAN BOATS, INC.
Highway 5 North, Route 3
Lebanon, Missouri 65536
Phone: (417) 532-7288

Osagian Boats, Inc., offers four models of cruising-type aluminum canoes—a 15-foot standard, a 16-foot square stern, a 17-foot standard, and a 17-foot whitewater.

These canoes feature rolled bulkheads and seats; three thwarts; enclosed flotation chambers at the ends; press-formed ribs (six in the standard models, seven in the whitewater models); heat-treated, stretch-formed 6061 skins tempered to T-6; and heliarc-welded canoe bottoms (a first, as far as we can determine).

OUIATENON CANOE COMPANY
228 De Hart
West Lafayette, Indiana 47906
Phone: (317) 743-3051

Ouiatenon Canoe Company builds two 13-foot 2-inch kayak models, the Fun One and the Sculpin. Both are touring-design boats constructed of a combination of fiberglass and nylon cloth and polyester resin, with triple seams. An Ethafoam seat rests on the bottom. This relieves a lot of the stresses imposed on decks by "hung seats," and it has also been found to be a lot more comfortable for the longer cruises. The company also makes a junior kayak.

Ouiatenon was founded in 1976 by four paddlers who began building boats for themselves. These four paddlers are still the main work force, so if you intend to buy from them, order well in advance.

The company also offers canoes by Pat Moore, We-No-Nah, Perception, and Michi-Craft, as well as canoe and kayak paddles and other accessories.

The sleek Fun One kayak turned out by Ouiatenon.

PAT MOORE CANOES, INC.
5256 East 65th Street
Indianapolis, Indiana 46220
Phone: (317) 849-9452

You haven't heard of Pat Moore Canoes, Inc.? Haven't seen many of their boats? Yes, you have—you just didn't know it.

Pat and his dad started building boats about 1970 under the name of Vega Integral Plastics. Under that name, they produced such boats as the Viper, the Venom, and the Canadian, boats that were years ahead of their time. The problem with company names is that somebody else always seems to pop up and claim he had it first, and so it was with Vega. So Pat and his dad shortened the name to V.I.P. Again, someone complained.

At this stage, Pat and his dad decided to play it safe. They named their company Moore Canoes, Inc., and added the Peter

Ouiatenon Canoe Company

Model	Length	Width	Weight	Price
Fun One	13'2"	24"	32 lb	$299
Sculpin	13'2"	—	—	$299
Junior	—	—	—	$225

The three thwarts of an Osagian canoe, plus the foam-filled chambers fore and aft, are visible in this photo.

Pond to their line. Then, disaster struck. In 1975, the factory burned to the ground—and with it the molds, the plans, and the equipment. Pat's dad decided to call it quits, but Pat opted to try again. In his usual manner, he has come up with some very good canoes.

All of the Moore canoes are hand-layup fiberglass cloth and woven roving with flexible polyester resin. (As is true for most good builders, the Moore formulas are secret.) The gunwales and thwarts are constructed of 6061 T-6 aluminum. The seats and decks are made of fiberglass.

Three models are offered at this time: the Egret, the Peter Pond II, and the Voyageur.

The Egret is a 14-footer which was designed expressly for single-handling but can also be used on quiet waters by two people. This is not a camping/cruising boat, but it is a very nice day-tripper.

The Peter Pond II is a 17-foot craft which was designed to be an all-around boat—a real family-type canoe. With its 30-inch-long decks, 1¼-inch rocker in the bow, and ½-inch rocker in the stern, this boat has good maneuvering characteristics and good speed.

The 18½-foot Voyageur was designed to get you, your partner, and quite a bit of

Pat Moore Canoes, Inc.

Model	Length	Beam at Gunwale	Weight	Depth	Capacity with Six Inches Freeboard
Egret	14'2''	35½''	52 lb	12''	450 lb
Peter Pond II	17'	35''	68 lb	13''	1,050 lb
Voyageur	18'6''	35''	83 lb	14½''	1,250 lb

camping gear from Point A to Point B fast and safely. Combining the best features of a racing craft with the best features of a good cruising boat, the Voyageur gives the buyer a lot for his money.

PERCEPTION, INC.
PO Box 64
Liberty, South Carolina 29657
Phone: (803) 859-7518

Perception offers two canoes made with ABS; three canoes constructed with fiberglass, nylon, and vinyl ester resin (one of which is decked); and three kayaks of fiberglass, nylon, and vinyl ester resin.

Perception has done extensive experimentation with vinyl ester resin. The company points out that this resin has been known and used for years in the chemical industry, but that because of its cost it did not become competitive with other resins until the energy crisis of 1974 increased the prices of the latter.

The Chattooga ABS is a whitewater canoe. The ABS hull is outfitted with rails of aluminum alloy fastened at four-inch intervals. There are eight structural cross braces, and there are also two cross braces under each seat. The double thwarts are ovaled. The end caps are of ABS.

The Nantahala ABS emphasizes wood fittings that are joined to the ABS hull. The rails are of seasoned hardwood, with stainless steel fasteners at five-inch intervals. The thwarts are of hickory, and the seats and end braces are also wooden. The wood is sealed with tung oil and coated with a urethane varnish. The end caps are of ABS.

The three canoes in fiberglass, nylon, and vinyl ester resin are the Keowee, the HD1, and the Warwoman C-1.

The Keowee is a 17-foot tripper which takes its design from wood-strip canoes. The seats are of rawhide, and the thwarts are of hickory. Like the hardwood of the Nantahala, the thwarts and other hardwood are protected with a tung oil sealant and a coat of urethane varnish.

Fast action in Perception canoe (left) and a Perception kayak (right).

Perception, Inc.

Model	Length	Width	Weight	Price
Chattooga	16'	33"	75 lb	$425
Nantahala	16'	33"	68 lb	$425
Keowee	17'	33"	60 lb	$399
HD1	13½'	28"	43 lb	$375
Warwoman C-1	13½'	28"	42 lb	$359
Spirit K-1	13'2"	23¾"	30 lb	$339
Victor K-1	13'2"	23¾"	32 lb	$339
Chauga K-1	13'2"	23¾"	32 lb	$339

The HD1 is a highly maneuverable 13½-foot racer that was designed for use by seasoned canoeists.

The Warwoman C-1, also a 13½-footer, is decked. It was designed to be very responsive for whitewater river running. The seat height is adjustable. The construction is the same as that of the company's kayaks.

The hulls of all the Perception kayaks contain an extra rib of graphite fibers. Each kayak has extra reinforcement in the ends and under the seat. The hulls are built without a gel coat and the decks have gel coat in assorted colors. The Perception kayaks are the Spirit, the Victor, and the Chauga.

The Spirit is a competition and river-running boat of low volume for paddlers below 145 pounds.

The Victor, a high-volume kayak, has good stability, a desirable feature for beginners. It can be bought with an extra-large seat.

The Chauga is a medium-volume kayak. It is a fast-turning boat, and, the company notes, it "tracks fair when on flat water."

PHOENIX PRODUCTS, INC.
U.S. Route 421
Tyner, Kentucky 40486
Phone: (606) 364-5141

Phoenix Products produces a line of good-quality kayaks for both the racer and the cruiser. A fiberglass/nylon lamination system and polyester resin are used in the construction of all of its craft. All of the Phoenix models feature a combination cockpit ring and seat hung from the deck (except for the Cascade II model), grab loops of ¼-inch diameter nylon rope, and a two-layer seam. The high quality of Phoenix boats is evidenced by the number of top paddlers who use the Slipper slalom kayak and the Match II downriver kayak in national and international competition.

The Slipper is a specialized slalom racing boat designed by ACA Commodore Chuck Tummonds in response to the need of U.S. paddlers for a highly competitive U.S.-made boat. The final design was settled upon after many designs were tried and rejected. The

Phoenix Products, Inc.

	Complete	Kit
Slipper	$375	$270
Savage	$375	$270
Cascade	$375	$270
Appalachian	$375	$270
Isere	$375	$270
Match II	$375	$270
Vagabond K-2	$550	NA
Cascade II	$290	NA

Slipper is an extremely good low-volume boat for the racer, but it is not recommended for the recreational paddler. You will undoubtedly see many such boats around, but unless you see the name "Phoenix" on the deck, the boat is probably a pirate model taken from an illegal mold. (Pirating of this kind is a very discouraging fact of life for many of the people who put in much time and money trying to help U.S. paddlers. You can do these creative people a favor by not purchasing any but authorized factory-built models. The prices are quite reasonable for the product you get.)

Another racing design is the Match II, a very fast, good-tracking kayak used by most of the top racers in the United States. Again, this boat is not recommended for the recreational paddler, and as with the Slipper, you may find "cheap" copies for sale.

The Savage is a slalom-design boat with good rocker, a small amount of V in the bow, and a good flat section in the center and toward the stern, and a good deal more volume than the Slipper. All of this makes the Savage a very maneuverable and stable boat for river running—a very good combination cruiser/racer.

The Cascade is similar to the Savage, but it has considerably more V in the hull and less rocker, making it a little faster and easier-tracking than the Savage. This boat was designed for the recreational paddler who wants a good, maneuverable, fast kayak with a little room for some gear. The Cascade II, an economy version of this model, is offered with a two-inch foam plank, and a limited color selection.

The Appalachian is a good, large-volume kayak with plenty of room for a large person or camping gear.

The Isere is a kind of compromise between the longer, faster Match downriver kayak and the Savage slalom-cruising kayak.

Five kayaks by Phoenix. From left: Match, Cascade II, Cascade, Appalachian, Isere.

It is an excellent boat for the recreational user who does most of his paddling on relatively flat stretches of rivers or on lakes. Because of its longer length, this boat easily outruns all of its brothers with the exception of the Match.

The Cascade is a two-person kayak designed for the kayaker who likes to have company when he is paddling but does not want to push a canoe. It is designed to be used on lakes, bays, and rivers, but advanced paddlers can also handle it in reasonably rough waters not requiring fairly sharp maneuvers.

PINETREE CANOES, LTD.
PO Box 824
Orillia, Ontario, Canada L3V 6K8
Phone: (705) 325-3233

Pinetree Canoes, Ltd., offers three basic models of canoes: the Abitibi in lengths of 14, 15, 16, and 17 feet; the Ojibwa 16-footer; and the Algonkin 14-footer. These canoes have hulls of Kevlar 49 Aramid fiber and epoxy resin, sitka spruce inwales, white ash out-wales, black cherry decks, maple thwarts, and rawhide seats. The care and attention given to the construction of the canoes is evidenced by their good looks and excellent light weight. (A 17-foot model capable of safely carrying 1,200 pounds weighs only 69 pounds.)

The Abitibi boats, with their broad beams (ranging from 36 to 39 inches) and their high carrying capacity (700 to 1,200 pounds), are good "tripping" canoes and especially so for voyages where portaging can be expected.

The Ojibwa boats, with their sharp, long bow and narrow beam (32 inches), are "sporting" canoes that have been designed for river running and racing.

The Algonkin is a single-person sport/cruising canoe with somewhat limited capacity.

Make no mistake about it—these canoes are expensive as compared to some of the others covered in this book. However, these canoes can be bounced off rocks and carried far and easily, which is more than can be said for most of the cheaper models. Thus, as noted earlier, you pay for what you get, and in this case you get a lot for what you pay.

An Ojibwa canoe by Pinetree being paddled solo.

Pinetree Canoes, Ltd.

Model and Construction	Length	Beam	Depth	Capacity Six-inch Freeboard	Approximate Weight	Price
14LW	14'	36''	12''	700 lb	35 lb	$730
15LW	15'	38''	13''	800 lb	39 lb	$780
15HD	15'	38''	13''	800 lb	43 lb	$830
16LW	16'	38''	13''	1,000 lb	41 lb	$875
16HD	16'	38''	13''	1,000 lb	48 lb	$925
17LW	17'	39''	15''	1,250 lb	55 lb	$1,090
17HD	17'	39''	15''	1,250 lb	59 lb	$1,295
17Y-ST LW	17'6''	39''	15''	1,250 lb	62 lb	$1,249
17Y-ST HD	17'6''	39''	15''	1,250 lb	69 lb	$1,395
Ojibwa LW	16'4''	32''	13''	450 lb	37 lb	$895
Ojibwa HD	16'4''	32''	13''	450 lb	43 lb	$955
Algonkin	13'8''	34''	11''	350 lb	33 lb	$695

QUAPAW CANOE COMPANY
600 Newman Road
Miami, Oklahoma 74354
Phone: (918) 542-5536

Quapaw Canoe Company offers seven fiberglass, one ABS Royalex, and four aluminum canoe models.

The company is owned by Richard Lillard, an avid and very good canoeist, who has designed into each of his boats the qualities that a paddler looks for.

All of the fiberglass canoes are laid up by hand, using fiberglass cloth, mat and roving, and polyester resin. (For those of you who want a strong, lighter-weight canoe for heavy river running, Quapaw can also build these models in Kevlar.) The gunwales and thwarts are of extruded aluminum, and the seats are bucket-type fiberglass. Built-in polystyrene flotation gives these canoes a natural upright floating characteristic when they are swamped. The Pioneer, Drake, and Guide models have a standard 3/4-inch-deep V keel, and the Challenger has a shallow or shoe keel which is about 3/16-inch deep. The other fiberglass models are flat, or keelless.

Fiberglass models are: the 12-foot, one-man Okie; the 15-foot, keelless Scout; the Pioneer, a 17-foot standard cruiser; the Guide, a 16-

Quapaw Canoe Company

Model	Length	Weight	Width	Depth	Capacity	Price
Morning Star	17'	69 lb	34 1/2''	12''	760 lb	$380
Okie	12'	47 lb	32''	12 1/2''	380 lb	$315
Guide	16'	73 lb	34''	12 1/2''	720 lb	$388
Drake	17'	91 lb	35 3/4''	12 1/2''	1,000 lb	$406
Challenger	17'	90 lb	35''	13 1/2''	780 lb	$415
Scout	15'	67 lb	33''	12 1/2''	670 lb	$365
Pioneer	17'	75 lb	35''	12 1/2''	780 lb	$388
17 Whitewater	17'	82 lb	37''	14''	780 lb	$419
17 Double End	17'	80 lb	37''	14''	780 lb	$388
16 Square Stern	16'	79 lb	37''	14''	700 lb	$419
15 Double End	15'	75 lb	36''	14''	690 lb	$368
Royalex	16'	74 lb			730 lb	$459

foot square-sterner; the Drake, a 17-foot square-sterner; the Challenger, a 17-foot model with extra reinforcing for whitewater paddling; and the Morning Star, a fast-design, lighter-weight 17-footer built to USCA requirements for racing in the cruiser class.

In ABS Royalex, Quapaw offers a 16-foot whitewater model called the Royalex.

The aluminum canoe line consists of the 17-foot Whitewater, which has seven ribs and a 3/8-inch shallow-draft interior keel; the 17-foot Standard, with six ribs and a standard keel; the 16-foot Square Stern, with six ribs; and the 15-foot Double End, with five ribs.

These canoes are all built with .051 heat-treated 6061-T6 aluminum, and they all feature welded hulls, extruded aluminum gunwales and thwarts, polystyrene flotation at the bow and the stern tanks, nonskid finish of the interior bottom, and rolled seat edges and bulkheads.

QUICKSILVER FIBERGLASS CANOES
Quicksilver Manufacturing, Ltd.
Box 104
Strome, Alberta, Canada T0B 4H0
Phone: (403) 376-3502

Quicksilver canoes are constructed of polyester-reinforced fiberglass mat, a woven roving, and mat layups, all done by hand. The exterior finish is done with a gel-coat resin. The gunwales are plastic-coated aluminum, and the thwarts are hardwood. The seat mounts are molded as part of the canoe hull and are provided with vinyl-covered, cushioned seat pads.

Quicksilver offers four 16-foot models and one 18-foot-model canoe. The QIV, one of the 16-foot canoes, is a square-stern model that is suitable for use with a motor of up to three-horsepower. The weights of these boats

indicate that a great deal of effort goes into the layup work to ensure that all excess resin is removed. Otherwise, the boats would certainly be 10 to 15 pounds heavier.

The QVII is probably the best model of this line for cruising, though its 90-pound weight would make portaging, or even carrying the canoe between the car and the river, a chore that a paddler would not want to do alone.

R.K.L.
Pretty Marsh
Mount Desert, Maine 04660

R.K.L. specializes in handmade cedar-strip canoes. Each canoe is built with 3/4-inch-wide by 1/4-inch-thick white cedar strips, covered inside and outside with four-ounce fiberglass cloth and epoxy resin over which a polyurethane, ultraviolet-protected clear marine varnish is painted. The gunwales, seats, and thwarts are made from spruce or ash, with nylon webbing for the seats (rawhide is optional). These boats not only are good-looking but are also strong and light (the River 18-footer weighs only 60 pounds).

R.K.L. produces two types of canoes—the River and the UGO. The River comes in lengths of 14, 16, 17, and 18 feet. The UGO, designed after the Rushton canoes, comes in lengths of 16 and 18 feet.

The River is a versatile craft. It is designed for one or two paddlers and for use as a "river running" or "tripping" canoe. Its light weight makes it easy to portage.

The UGO, with its V hull and its 32-inch width, is more suited to lakes and bays, where its shape makes it ideal for windy and rough conditions.

For those of you who have something special in mind, R.K.L. will also build custom designs.

Quicksilver Fiberglass Canoes

Model	QII	QIII	QIV	QVI	QVII
Length	16'	16'	16'	16'	18'
Width	35"	34"	36"	31"	35"
Depth	13"	12"	14"	14"	16"
Weight	70 lb	65 lb	85 lb	70 lb	90 lb
Capacity	850 lb	650 lb	825 lb	650 lb	950 lb

R.K.L.

	Length	Width	Depth	Weight*	Displacement	Price
River						
	14'	32"	13"	40 lb	450 lb	$770
	16'	34"	13"	48 lb	750 lb	$810
	17'	34"	13"	52 lb	900 lb	$830
	18'	36"	13"	60 lb	1,100 lb	$850
UGO						
	16'	32"	13"	45 lb	700 lb	$810
	18'	32"	13"	58 lb	1,000 lb	$850

*Canoe weights are calculated with the use of four-ounce polypropylene cloth, epoxy resin, and spruce wood in the seats, thwarts, and gunwales.

As with all boats of this type, delivery is not going to be fast, so you should order in the fall for the following season.

A cedar-strip canoe made by R.K.L. (Robert K. Lincoln) in Maine.

SAWYER CANOE COMPANY
234 South State Street
Oscoda, Michigan 48750
Phone: (517) 739-9181

The Sawyer Canoe Company manufactures three basic canoe lines in fiberglass and Kevlar.

The top line is named the Sawyer. Boats in this line are made by a hand-layup of woven fiberglass cloth and tooling-grade polyester resin.

Canoes in the AuSable line look like their counterparts in the Sawyer line. However, their construction is of chopped fiberglass, with an inside layer of woven roving and tooling-grade polyester resin. (These boats are slightly heavier than the boats in the Sawyer line, and not quite as strong, but they are considerably less expensive.)

The Yankee Rebels are the "Volkswagen" line. They are made of standard-grade polyester resin and chopped fiberglass, with an inside layer of woven roving. They are available in only one color and in two lengths. They are designed for casual outings such as fishing or lake camping.

The Rebels are designed primarily for non-canoeists. The longer of the two, 16 feet long and 36 inches wide, is a very forgiving boat for beginners or youngsters on fairly calm water. It is not designed for use on rough water.

The Sawyer line includes the Sport, the Charger, the Champion III, the Super, the Saber, the Safari, the Guide Special, and the Canadian.

The Sport, a 16-foot-long, 36-inch-wide model, is designed for camping, fishing, or just paddling on lakes or quiet rivers. It is also available in the AuSable line.

The Charger, an 18½-foot model, is designed for use as a whitewater racer in the open-canoe class and also as a cruiser. In the proper hands, this very swift craft can also be used to run whitewater.

At the top is the Sawyer Champion, a five-time winner of the USCA National Championships. At the bottom is the Sawyer Guide Special, operating under sizable load amid the spectacular scenery of Jackson Hole, Wyoming.

The Champion is a full-blown, 18½-foot-long racing canoe, which has won the USCA National Championships five times. This canoe is OK for the advanced paddler who wants more zip for cruising than is found in standard boats, but it does take some getting used to.

The Super is another 18½-foot-long boat that is designed for the professional canoe racer. Like the Champion, this craft makes a nice cruiser for the "retired" racer, but it is definitely not for the novice paddler.

The Saber, 24 feet long, is an out-and-out racing canoe with a hull speed that is greater than most paddlers are capable of pushing it at. It was designed for the Unlimited racing class, and as such it is a single-purpose canoe.

The Safari is an 18-foot square-sterner that is designed to carry an outboard motor of up to five horsepower.

The Guide Special is a fast and stable general-purpose canoe that is designed to carry heavy loads of gear for tripping and camping. It is also offered in the AuSable line.

The Canadian is a 16½-foot lightweight canoe, with good depth. It is designed for whitewater racing in the open-canoe class or for just cruising.

Most of the company's canoes are offered in Kevlar at much less weight than the fiberglass canoes, but also at considerably more money. As has been mentioned earlier in this book, the benefits of Kevlar are worth the money to racers, but the "average" canoeist can get along just fine with fiberglass.

SEA NYMPH MANUFACTURING
PO Box 298
Syracuse, Indiana 46567
Phone: (219) 457-3131

Sea Nymph offers 22 models of aluminum canoes constructed of 6061 marine aluminum heat-treated to a T-6 temper. The gunwales and keels are built of extruded aluminum. The thwarts are of seamless aluminum tubing. Inner-outer keels are standard on all models. Except for the 15CX, the 17CX and the 186M Marauder, all models have aluminum ribs. All models feature polystyrene foam flotation in bulkheads in the bow and the stern, and tie shackles of stainless steel at each end.

Sea Nymph sends potential buyers literature which fully explains its methods of construction and includes pictures of its canoes. However, the company's specification chart must be read a couple of times in order to figure out how the boats are classified.

Models range in length from 13 feet to 18½ feet and in width from 34 inches to 42 inches.

The standard canoe models are the 13-foot 13C, the 15-foot 15C, and the 17-foot 17C. Although of standard-weight construction, these canoes are designed for fairly heavy use.

The lightweight models are the 15CL and

Sawyer Canoe Company

Model	Length	Beam	Depth	Capacity	Fiberglass		Kevlar	
					Weight	Price	Weight	Price
Sawyer								
Sport*	16'	36"	13"	640 lb	63 lb	$370	45 lb	$570
Guide Special*	18'	36"	13"	890 lb	78 lb	$420	56 lb	$620
Cruiser	17'9"	33"	12½"	649 lb	68 lb	$410	47 lb	$610
Super	18'6"	33"	11"	757 lb	62 lb	$420	39 lb	$620
Safari	18'	36"	13"	968 lb	80 lb	$430	68 lb	$630
Canadian*	16'6"	33"	14"	760 lb	67 lb	$390	43 lb	$590
Champion III	18'6"	30"	11½"	695 lb	68 lb	$420	39 lb or 46 lb	$620
Charger	18'6"	31"	14½"	1,078 lb	82 lb	$460	67 lb	$710
Saber	24'	26"	11½"	500 lb	59 lb	$455	35 lb	$655
AuSable								
Sport	16'	36"	13"	640 lb	70 lb	$290		
Guide Special	18'	36"	13"	890 lb	85 lb	$330		
Cruiser	17'9"	33"	12½"	649 lb	75 lb	$320		
Yankee								
Rebel 16'	16'	36"	13½"	640 lb	72 lb	$199		
Rebel 13'	13'	36"	13"	600 lb	59 lb	$183	44 lb	$570

*These three Sawyer models now have increased depth and load-carrying capacity. The Sport and the Canadian have also been increased in length.

the 17CL. As with all Sea Nymph models, the lengths are indicated by the model numbers.

The whitewater models are the 15CW and the 17CW. These boats have the same skin thickness as the standard models but feature flush rivets and a two-piece shallow-draft keel. Such craft are also referred to as shallow-draft canoes.

The standard "livery" canoes—the 15CX and the 17CX models—have an extra-heavy keel and flush rivets.

The Supersport 14C and the Sportsman 16C are square-sterners for use with outboard motors of up to five horsepower.

The 186M Marauder is an 18½-foot "limited edition" canoe. Constructed of .040-gauge aluminum, this craft comes out at a nice, light 65 pounds.

Sea Nymph Manufacturing

Model	Width	Depth	Capacity	Weight	Price
13C	42"	13¾"	600 lb	62 lb	$315
15C	36⅛"	13¾"	660 lb	70 lb	$324
17C	37"	13¾"	800 lb	79 lb	$350
15CL	36⅛"	13¾"	660 lb	63 lb	$335
17CL	37"	13¾"	800 lb	70 lb	$370
15CW	36⅛"	13¾"	660 lb	71 lb	$350
17CW	37"	13¾"	800 lb	80 lb	$390
15CX	36⅛"	13¾"	660 lb	72 lb	$350
17CX	37"	13¾"	800 lb	82 lb	$390
14C	38"	14"	665 lb	81 lb	$380
16C	37"	13¾"	765 lb	78 lb	$360
186M	34"	11½"		65 lb	$595

SEDA PRODUCTS
PO Box 997
Chula Vista, California 92010
Phone: (714) 425-3222

Seda is a nine-year-old company specializing in racing and cruising kayaks and canoes. All Seda kayaks are built of hand-layup fiberglass and polyester resin (tooling grade), with Kevlar-polyester models available at higher prices. Except for the Royalex, which is constructed of ABS Royalex, the canoes are put together in the same manner as the kayaks.

The racing kayak models include the Strike, a slalom kayak with an extremely low volume, and the Spirit, a downriver kayak.

The Cobra is a slalom double racing canoe, which can also be used for cruising.

The Vagabond is a cruising kayak which is similar to a slalom kayak in looks and behavior but is a foot longer and a little wider, making it very comfortable for cruising.

The Explorer is a partially decked cruising canoe with a large open cockpit (from the front seat to the rear seat). This opening can be covered with an optional spray cover which has two sewn-in cones to permit the entry of paddlers. Fiberglass seats are provided, as is foam flotation in the bow and the stern.

The Wanderer is a 17½-foot fiberglass open canoe designed for cruising. It features cane seats and mahogany gunwales, thwarts, and end caps. For those who care about weight and are willing to spend the extra money, a hybrid Kevlar-fiberglass construction is also available.

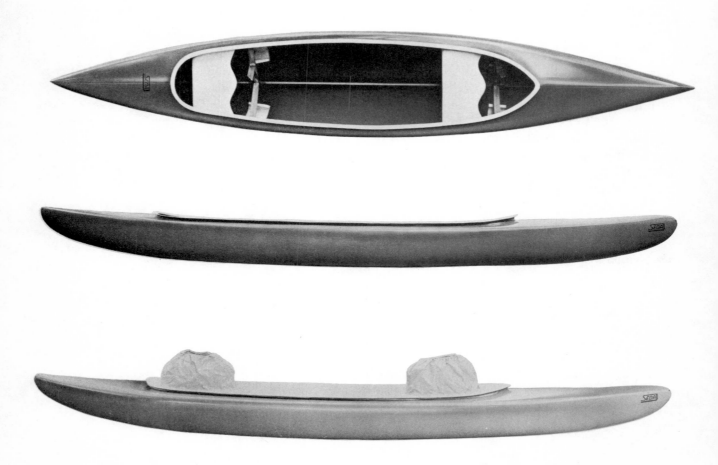

Three views of Seda's fifteen-foot Explorer. The bottom view shows the spray cover fitted and the two cones (spray skirts) ready for paddlers.

Seda Products

Model	Length	Beam	Depth	Capacity	Price
Kayaks					
Strike	13'2"	24"	10"	200 lb	$350
Spirit	14'9"	24"	14"	250 lb	$375
Vagabond	14'	25"	13"	350 lb	$299
Dart	13'2"	24"	13"	300 lb	$299
Seasurf	9'6"				$299
Canoes					
Explorer	15'	33"			$399
Wanderer	17½'	36"	14"		$428
Royalex	16'	35"	14"		$448
Cobra	15'	32"			$399
Orion	13'2"				$375

For the single racer and cruiser, Seda offers the Mamba, a single slalom canoe with good volume and low ends for gate sneaking. The boat comes with a plastic molded seat, grab loops, and aluminum knee braces ready for installation.

The Seasurf is a 9½-foot kayak designed for paddling in the heavy surf of the Pacific Ocean.

SEVYLOR USA, INC.
6279 East Slauson, Suite 407
Los Angeles, California 90040
Phone: (213) 728-7877

Sevylor is a major manufacturer of inflatable boats that range from the Tahiti line of kayaks to the Caravelle line of rafts to the K68 and K88 powered runabouts.

Sevylor USA, Inc.

Caravelle round boats

Model	Price
K 16 Child	$ 11.50
K 26 Junior	$ 16.50
K 36 1 Man	$ 30.00
K 56 2 Man	$ 50.00
K 66 3 Man	$ 65.00
K 76 4 Man	$100.00
K 86 4 Man	$116.50
K106 4 Man	$125.00
K116 5 Man	$150.00
K105 4 Man	$133.25
K115 5 Man	$166.75

A Tahiti GT sport model by Sevylor barrels through whitewater with two kayak paddles flashing. The fabric used in this model has a 25 percent heavier gauge than the fabric used in the Tahiti K77.

Tahiti kayaks

Model	Price
K 37 Junior	$ 33.25
K 57 1 Man	$ 58.25
K 67 2 Man	$ 91.75
K 77 2 Man	$116.75
K107 3 Man	$158.25
K 79 2 Man	$166.75
K109 2 Man Deluxe	$191.75
GT-69 Jerry Bentley	$159.95
GT-79 Jerry Bentley	$166.75

The Tahiti kayaks range in size from the K37 Junior model to the GT79 Jerry Bentley and the new K79 and K109 models, which feature heavier-gauge in hull and deck materials for rougher usage. They have 13 independent air chambers.

The Caravelle series is a line of rafts that range in capacity from one child to four adults plus a child. The Caravelles can be rowed, paddled, powered, or sailed. Three-chamber construction enables a Caravelle to stay afloat if a chamber gets punctured.

The runabouts come in two models—the K69, 9 feet 2 inches long, which is designed to carry two people and to be powered with an outboard motor of up to six horsepower; and the K88, 11 feet long, which can carry three people and can be operated with an outboard motor of up to ten horsepower.

SIERRA CANOES
735 Riverview
Orange, California 92665
Phone: (714) 637-4166

Sierra Canoes offers two fiberglass open canoes, the 16-foot Sierra Classic and the 15-foot Woodsman.

The hulls are constructed of fiberglass cloth and polyester resin; oak and mahogany are used for the gunwales, the thwarts, and the decks. Both canoes feature flat, wide floors and extra fullness in the bow and the stern for higher riding in rough water.

The ends of the Sierra Classic are the classic Indian design. The Woodsman's ends are relatively low for less wind resistance.

The sixteen-foot Daron (top) and the sixteen-foot Micmac (bottom), two canoes made by 6-H Products.

Sierra Canoes

Model	Length	Width	Depth	Weight	Capacity	Price
Sierra Classic	16'	36''	13''	72 lb	700 lb	$425
Woodsman	15'	33''	12''	60 lb	500 lb	$385

6-H Products, Ltd.

Model	Length	Width	Weight	Capacity	Price
Daron	16'	35''	60 lb	800 lb	$400
Daron	14'	34''	50 lb	600 lb	$350
Micmac	16'	33''	65 lb	800 lb	$400
C-1	17'	29''	36 lb	200 lb	$400

6-H PRODUCTS, LTD.
80 Hickson Avenue
Kingston, Ontario, Canada
Phone: (613) 546-4923

6-H Products, Ltd., offers two open cruising canoes (the Darons), one whitewater canoe (the Micmac), and one racing canoe (the C-1).

All four boats are built of fiberglass-reinforced plastic and are of foam-sandwich construction, with integral decks, gunwales, and thwarts.

All models are also offered in a Kevlar-foam sandwich, with a weight reduction of about 10 percent and a price increase of about 20 percent.

STARCRAFT COMPANY
2703 College Avenue
Goshen, Indiana 46526
Phone: (219) 533-0481

Starcraft is a major builder of aluminum canoes. It doesn't offer many models, but those that it does offer are turned out well.

Construction is of stretch-formed 6061-T6 marine aluminum, with an extruded aluminum keel and extruded aluminum gunwales, aluminum pan seats, and aluminum tube thwarts. All parts are riveted; flathead rivets are used in the hull, and roundhead rivets are used along the gunwales, seats, and thwarts. All models have aluminum interior ribs (four in the Sequoia 15, five in the others).

A sponson section runs longitudinally along each boat at the waterline from a point near the foredeck back to the rear seat. This section is designed to give the boat added stability in rough water.

The Sequoia 15 is a 15-foot model for one or two people. The Sioux 16 is a 16-foot square-stern model suitable for two people

plus camping gear. The Seneca 17 is a 17-foot model. The Iroquois 17 is a 17-foot canoe with a flat keel, a reinforced bow, and an optional spray cover.

SUNSPOT PLASTICS, INC.
2453 Dixie Road
Mississauga, Ontario, Canada L4Y 2A1
Phone: (416) 272-0552

Sunspot Plastics builds the Sunchief line of canoes. These are constructed of polyethylene

The Seneca 17 by Starcraft takes a young family through quiet water and a sylvan setting.

plastics and feature a one-piece hull, anodized aluminum gunwales, a full-length center keel and two keelsons for added strength and stability, and Ethafoam sponsons along the gunwales and Styrofoam under the seats for flotation.

Starcraft Company

Model	Width	Depth	Weight	Capacity	Price
Sequoia 15	37½"	13"	70 lb	635 lb	$336
Sioux 16	36¼"	13"	79 lb	740 lb	$378
Seneca 17	36¼"	13"	78 lb	755 lb	$355
Iroquois 17	36¼"	13"	78 lb	755 lb	$390

Sunspot Plastics, Inc.

Model	Width	Depth	Weight	Capacity	Price
14-footer	37''	14''	60 lb	600 lb	$299
16-footer	37''	14''	68 lb	750 lb	$319

THOMPSON CANOE COMPANY
Box 2
Hairy Hill, Alberta, Canada T0B 1S0

Thompson Canoe Company is a very small firm specializing in canoes of wood and canvas. Since it only builds 35 to 40 canoes a year, you would need to place your order well ahead of the paddling season. Most boats are built to individual order.

Thompson canoes are constructed of clear, straight-grained cedar planking; sitka spruce ribs; white oak gunwales, thwarts, and seat frames (the seats are laced with rawhide); and brass or copper fastenings. The covering is No. 8 canvas filled with white lead and coated with marine enamel.

All Thompson canoes are hand-built, with one person doing the entire job from start to finish.

TIP-A-CANOE STORES, INC.
Route 2, Box 87E
Kingston Springs, Tennessee 37082
Phone: (615) 797-2674

Tip-A-Canoe Stores, Inc., offers a 16-foot ABS Royalex whitewater canoe with aluminum gunwales and thwarts, fiberglass seats, and aluminum sheet deck plates.

VOYAGEUR CANOE COMPANY, LTD.
King Street
Milbrook, Ontario, Canada L0A 1G0
Phone: (705) 932-2131

Voyageur builds nine canoe models, ranging in length from 12 feet to 36 feet. They are constructed of hand-layup fiberglass cloth and polyester resin, with premolded epoxy ribs built in for added rigidity and strength, red

Thompson Canoe Company

Model	Width	Depth	Weight	Capacity	Price
Standard 16 foot	34½''	13½''	70 lb	800 lb	$630
Standard 18 foot	35''	13½''	80 lb	950 lb	$705

Tip-A-Canoe Stores, Inc.

Model	Length	Width	Weight	Capacity	Price
Spear-Craft	16'2''	36''	75 lb	700 lb	$390

Voyageur Canoe Company, Ltd.

Model	Length	Width	Depth	Weight	Capacity	Price
Montreal	36'	70''	24''	387 lb	4,250 lb	$4,380
North Country	25'	44''	19''	278 lb	2,700 lb	$2,480
Outer	21'	44''	18''	185 lb	2,250 lb	$1,180
Traveller	18'	33''	13''	72 lb	900 lb	$ 555
Nor'Wester	17'	36''	16''	87 lb	1,100 lb	$ 588
Tripper	16'	36''	13''	64 lb	860 lb	$ 443
Guide	14'	34''	13''	52 lb	675 lb	$ 378
Scout	12'	35''	12''	39 lb	540 lb	$ 302
Trapper	12'	26''	12''	30 lb	350 lb	$ 266

oak gunwales, and white ash decks. Flotation is provided by foam-filled chambers in the bow and the stern. The seats are built with white ash frames and woven nylon webbing.

The Scout, a lightweight 12-footer for hunters and fishermen, is strictly a one-person design.

The Trapper, like the Scout, is a lightweight 12-foot design. However, because of its narrower width it has less carrying capacity.

The Tripper, a 16-foot canoe, is designed for tripping, cruising, or running whitewater.

The Nor'Wester is a 17-foot model whose 36-inch width and 16-inch depth make it a good cargo carrier. You should remember, however, that its capacity is based on six inches of freeboard, which means that the boat is ten inches down in the water and could prove to be quite unstable under rough water conditions. Still, this boat has to be considered seriously by people who make long trips.

The Traveller is a nice, fast 18-footer with a beam that is somewhat narrow for heavy water. In lakes and rivers, however, its length and low profile should make the miles go by easily.

The Outer is a 21-foot canoe with very good stability and carrying capacity. Wildlife centers used it quite extensively for touring and excursions.

The 25-foot North Country and the 36-foot Montreal are craft designed primarily for use by camps and large groups, such as Scout troops. These canoes are paddled by six to ten people. They have a high-density foam lamination for additional buoyancy.

Voyageur also offers an extensive line of wood paddles.

WABASH VALLEY CANOES
506 Road 225 West
Crawfordsville, Indiana 47933
Phone: (317) 362-3538

If you have your perfect canoe in mind but can't find it, or if you need a superfast racing canoe or just a very nice cruising canoe, call Bob Demoret of Wabash Valley Canoes.

Bob is a super craftsman who uses top-quality materials (fiberglass, Kevlar, Kev-Glass, other things) and techniques to build top-quality boats. Most of his boats are racers, and these are built to be tough and fast. His cruisers are fast and tough too, but they are also stable.

The Demoret C-1 and C-2 USCA Racers are designed and built for one purpose—to get the paddler from the start to the finish of a race ahead of everybody else. These are not docile boats, and they should be considered

Voyageur's eighteen-foot Traveller, a fast canoe with a low profile.

only by racers or by paddlers who are getting into racing.

The C-4 Olympic is likewise an out-and-out flatwater racing craft.

The Explorer is a 16-footer that has been designed to make fun out of paddling in rough water. Its bow and stern are high and wide for lifting over waves, and it has been built to take the abuse given to it in rental service from outfitters.

The 18½-foot Whitewater Cruiser is what Bob calls his "all-around canoe." It has good handling characteristics, space and carrying capacity for gear, and a nice glide, making it well suited both for use on lakes and as a whitewater cruiser.

If you want a kayak, you can still call Bob. When we last saw him, he had several kayak designs floating around, but since Bob's first love is canoes, his kayaks have to be asked for.

If you want to try out one of Bob's boats, before you decide, you can do that too, since he runs river trips right near his shop.

WE-NO-NAH CANOES
PO Box 247
Winona, Minnesota 55987
Phone: (507) 454-5430

We-No-Nah is the prime builder of Jensen-design canoes, famous throughout the United States and Canada for their racing records.

These hand-layup boats are constructed of fiberglass, Kevlar, fiberglass and nylon, and Kevlar and nylon—depending on the model and the wishes of the purchaser. All models come with fiberglass seats and aluminum gunwales and thwarts.

The models include racers, cruiser/racers, professional racers, and whitewater canoes. These boats are not designed for the novice or the beginning paddler, but are aimed at the advanced user who wants to put a little excitement into his paddling.

The boats range in length from 14 feet to 18½ feet. The accompanying table is based on a company description.

We-No-Nah Canoes

Prices

18½' USCA Jensen Cruiser
Lightweight model—"skin coat" of new PVC-core construction; adjustable stern foot brace and sliding bow seat; weight: approximately 46 lb. ... $475

Standard-weight model—center-rib construction; adjustable stern foot brace and sliding bow seat; weight: approximately 59 lb. ... $420

Optional 9-inch adjustable sliding stern seat for above models. ... $ 18

18' Jensen Stock—meets USCA standard division specifications
Lightweight model—new PVC-core construction; weight: approximately 54 lb. ... $420
Standard-weight model—cross-rib construction; weight: approximately 62 lb. ... $380
Standard-weight model—center-rib construction; weight: approximately 67 lb. ... $380
Optional 15-inch adjustable sliding bow seat for above models ... $ 18

17' We-no-nah
Lightweight model—new PVC-core construction; weight: approximately 54 lb ... $380
Standard-weight model—cross-rib construction; weight: approximately 65 lb ... $320
Standard-weight model—center-rib construction; weight: approximately 68 lb ... $320

16½' We-no-nah
Standard-weight model—cross-rib construction; weight: approximately 64 lb ... $249

16' Jensen C-1
Lightweight model—"skin coat" core construction; weight: approximately 35 lb ... $310

14' Jensen C-1
Lightweight model—"skin coat" core construction; weight: approximately 30 lb ... $295

18½' Built-up Jensen or the new 18½' Jensen Whitewater II
Standard-weight model with nylon-reinforced layup—center-rib construction; weight: approximately 63 lb . $435

16½' Jensen Whitewater
Standard-weight model with nylon-reinforced layup—center-rib construction; weight: approximately 58 lb . $375

We-no-nah's 18½-foot Whitewater II cruising with small children aboard.

Spray skirt of nylon ($18.95) mounted on the White Brothers kayak.

WHITE BROTHERS
Box 845
Niagara Falls, New York 14302
Phone: (416) 262-4644

(also: Box 251
St. Davids, Ontario, Canada L0S 1P0)

White Brothers offers the buyer just one choice—a kayak called the Whitewater. It is a 13-foot, one-piece polyethylene cruising kayak. The lines of this boat are similar to those of the standard slalom kayak but have considerably more volume. The Whitewater weighs 40 pounds and costs $258. Foot braces are extra at $18.95 a set.

WHITEWATER BOATS
PO Box 483
Cedar City, Utah 84720
Phone: (801) 586-3109

Whitewater Boats offers 12 models of kayaks and canoes.

These boats are constructed of four hand-layup layers of ten-ounce cloth and tooling resin, with two additional layers in the bow and the stern of the kayaks and the whitewater canoes. In addition, three layers are placed in the deck just behind the cockpit, to resist crushing during entry and exit.

The Salmon, the Wenatchee, and the Clearwater each have five layers of cloth in the hull. The Surf kayaks and the Columbia K-2 have roving added to the hulls and decks for extra strength and rigidity. The kayaks feature adjustable, removable seats and adjustable footrests. Each of the kayaks and the canoes has an extra hole in the bow through which a bicycle cable lock can be used to lock it to a vehicle or a tree.

The kayak models are the Bronco, the Salmon, the Lochsa, the Arkansas, the Clearwater, and the Columbia.

The Bronco, designed by Tom Johnson, is a slalom kayak of intermediate volume and good turning characteristics.

The Salmon is a large-volume slalom kayak that can carry a 200-pound person and still have good turning characteristics. It is considered to be a little trickier than the Bronco, and it is recommended for the more experienced boater.

The Lochsa is a small-volume, heavy-water kayak whose hull is very similar to the Salmon's.

The Arkansas is a big-volume kayak that can be paddled comfortably by a person weighing 250 pounds. The cockpit is slightly oversized, and rudder kits can be purchased by those who do most of their paddling on deep, flat water.

The Clearwater is strictly a flat-water cruising kayak. It has been designed to be fast and stable on flat water even when it is loaded down with camping gear. A rudder kit for this boat is also available.

The Columbia, a two-person kayak, has been designed for flat-water or wild-water touring. The cockpits are spaced six feet apart so that you can roll without taking off your partner's head. When equipped with the optional rudder kit, this is a very nice touring kayak.

The Wenatchee is a touring/slalom, decked, one-person canoe designed for touring on the wild rivers out West. It has also been used successfully in slalom racing.

The Bean is a modified older-design slalom C-1 which has had its cockpit enlarged so that it can be paddled by two people. (The original design goes back to the days when the ICF rules said that the ends had to be higher than the cockpit.) This boat should be pretty cozy.

The Hoback is a 15-foot open canoe that has been designed for whitewater paddling. It features oak gunwales and thwarts. Cane seats are available at extra cost.

The Snake, like the Hoback, is laid up with 13 layers of fiberglass cloth in its bottom. At a length of 17 feet 2 inches, this boat is plenty fast. Yet it is also very stable and handy in whitewater and on lakes and rivers. The Snake features oak gunwales and thwarts, with cane seats offered at extra cost. Fiberglass bucket-type seats are standard.

The Shoe is a surfing kayak designed by Tom Johnson. It is quite stable, yet very maneuverable, and it is quite capable of doing end-overs, 360-degree turns and S-turns across the faces of a wave.

The Porpoise is a very fast and responsive high-performance competition surfing kayak.

Also available are the Jensen C-1 and the Jensen Wildwater Cruiser, at 14 feet and 18½ feet, respectively.

YUKON BOAT WORKS
1500 West North Avenue
Milwaukee, Wisconsin 53205

Yukon Boat Works produces 11 models of aluminum canoes in lengths of 15, 16, and 17 feet, in both heat-treated and standard types of aluminum.

ZODIAC OF NORTH AMERICA, INC.
11 Lee Street
Annapolis, Maryland 21401
Phone: (301) 268-2009

Zodiac, one of the leading builders of inflatable boats, started out in 1896—building airships. In 1936 the firm created the first inflatable boat, a craft that could be propelled by

Two kayaks by Whitewater Boats, the Clearwater (front) and the Salmon (rear), show off their lines in calm water.

Yukon Boat Works

	Double End				Square Stern			Double End			
	H-15	R-15	C-15	K-15	H-16	R-16	C-16	H-17	R-17	C-17	K-17
Type of aluminum	Heat-treated	Standard	Heat-treated	Heat-treated	Heat-treated	Standard	Heat-treated	Heat-treated	Standard	Heat-treated	Heat-treated
L.O.A.	15'	15'	15'	15'	16'	16'	16'	17'	17'	17'	17'
Beam	37"	37"	37"	37"	36"	36"	36"	36"	36"	36"	36"
Depth amidships	13"	13"	13"	13"	13"	13"	13"	13"	13"	13"	13"
Weight	69 lb	69 lb	69 lb	70 lb	75 lb	75 lb	75 lb	78 lb	78 lb	78 lb	79 lb
Capacity	660 lb	660 lb	660 lb	660 lb	795 lb	795 lb	795 lb	780 lb	780 lb	780 lb	780 lb
Prices	$329	$299	$345	$375	$375	$350	$395	$350	$329	$375	$400

either a canoe paddle or a kayak blade. In 1952 Alain Bombard crossed the Atlantic Ocean in a Zodiac Mark III.

A Zodiac basically consists of from two to five inflatable hull sections, an inflatable keel, wooden or aluminum floorboards, and an aluminum transom. The hull sections are constructed of densely woven nylon fabric impregnated with neoprene and hypalon. The top and bottom of the wooden floorboards are constructed of ash framing and marine mahogany plywood, with a polyurethane foam filler in between. This gives the floor good rigidity and strength without a weight penalty.

The purchaser of a Zodiac doesn't have to go shopping for the accessories that are needed to make it usable. These boats come complete with floorboards, an inflatable keel, two collapsible oars, oarlocks and rests, a transom pod, a sprayhood (except with the Junior model), carrying handles on the bow and sides, D-rings for attaching a cover, two carrying bags, and foot bellows with a hose and repair kit—everything you need (except life jackets) to get into the fun of boating.

Zodiacs are basically powered craft (horsepower ratings vary from 4 or 6 to 115), but they also make nice sailing or rowing craft.

The Cadet, a highly maneuverable 9-foot 10-inch boat, is said by the company to be ideal for campers and also useful as a tender.

Mark I, a 10-foot 6-inch model, can carry four people and is designed for use with motors ranging from 4 HP to 25 HP (to 10 HP in Mark I Junior, to 25 HP in Mark I DeLuxe).

Mark II Compact, a 12-foot 6-inch model, can carry five or six people and is designed for

Zodiac's Mark III Grand Raid (top) and Cadet (bottom) are being powered by Mercury outboard.

use with motors ranging from 6 HP to 40 HP.

Mark II Old Faithful, a 13-foot 10-inch model, can carry six people and is designed for use with motors ranging from 9½ HP to 55 HP.

Mark III, a 15-foot 5-inch model, can carry

up to ten people and is designed for use with motors ranging from 9½ HP to 65 HP. The manufacturer rates this boat suitable for use on open water.

Mark IV GR, a 17-foot 6-inch model, can carry up to 12 people or 2,750 pounds of cargo and is designed for use with motors ranging from 15 HP to 85 HP. It has been used on such rivers as the Rio Grande, the Yukon, the Congo, the Niger, and the Colorado, and even in the polar seas.

Tender IV and Tender VI are four- and six-man models, 9 feet 4 inches and 10 feet 2 inches long, respectively. These lightweight craft are easy to assemble and operate. Their good carrying capacity, 880 pounds and 950 pounds, respectively, makes them useful for many purposes. Both boats can be operated with motors of up to four horsepower.

You You is a 7-foot 3-inch two- or three-man life-raft type of craft that is designed to be rowed. Despite its small size, it can carry up to 500 pounds.

Mark V Heavy Duty is the largest craft of the Zodiac line. It is 19 feet ½ inch long, and it is capable of carrying up to 15 persons or up to 3,900 pounds of cargo. It can be operated with motors ranging from 70 HP to 115 HP. Amazingly enough, however, this boat weighs only 465 pounds.

Zodiac of North America, Inc.

Model	Type	Price
You You	0109	$578
Dinghy	0509	$804
Tender IV	0505	$635
Tender VI	1505	$795
Cadet	1119	$799
Mark I Junior	1217	$999
Mark I De Luxe	1247	$1,280
Mark II Compact	2245	$1,647
Mark II	2259	$1,940
Mark II GR	2355	$2,400
Mark III	3269	$2,556
Mark III GR	3463	$3,387
Mark IV GR	4375	$4,226
Mark V HD	5483	$6,170

5

Paddles, Poles,
and Other Means of Locomotion

There are two major means of propelling canoes and kayaks—paddles and poles.

Canoe paddles propel canoes. Kayak paddles propel kayaks. Poles—an old means of locomotion that is making a comeback—are used for canoes.

In the vernacular of racing, and sometimes in more formal usage as well, kayakers often refer to the instruments they use, not as "paddles" but as "blades." We were tempted to follow suit, but ultimately did not because we wished to avoid the ambiguity that arises if you sometimes use the word *blade* to mean the entire instrument and sometimes to mean the scoop—or the part that enters the water and is attached to a shaft.

Paddles come in a variety of materials. They may be all wood or all fiberglass; they may have an aluminum shaft and a paddle portion of another material; they may be of fiberglass over wood or over a foam core; or they may have a fiberglass shaft formed over a cardboard tube. They are also made of polystyrene. Such paddles are low in cost and are used primarily by outfitters who make rentals, where the loss rate is high.

Manufactured poles are made primarily of fiberglass or aluminum. Some home-made poles are of wood.

Canoe Paddles

Canoe paddles come in a variety of designs, lengths, and materials. Some of them have lines as clean as those of a Thoroughbred horse. The shafts of such paddles are meticulously formed to fit the hands, with T-grips at the top and a very efficient blade (or scoop) design at the bottom. Other shafts are bulkier and do not have a T at the top, but instead flare out to form a grip. A third type of shaft is simply rounded off at the top to form a pole-type end.

The size of the paddle blade ranges from

about 6 inches wide and 18 inches long to the "pizza type" used in marathon racing, which is up to 12 or 14 inches wide and about 12 to 14 inches long.

There is no formula that will tell you what paddle is best for your canoe and your uses. The best way is to try out several and get what you like. A racing type (the type with the lines of a Thoroughbred) would not be right for a lake or heavy whitewater, nor would the pizza type, because it requires too much exertion.

Canoe paddles usually range in length from four to six feet, with some home-made ones even longer. The four-foot length is usually considered right for children, and the six-foot length is about ideal for Olympic-type racing canoes.

The right length for the individual can well be determined as follows: When three-fourths of the paddle is in the water, with the user seated or kneeling and the paddle vertical, the hand that is on top of the shaft should be at about eye level. If the paddle is longer than this, using it will be unnecessarily fatiguing. If it is shorter, the paddler's body cannot be employed to full effectiveness. Racers generally find this formula ideal. However, a canoeist who is not in good physical condition should get a paddle that is one to two inches shorter than this, in order to reduce productive effort.

The weight of a paddle varies with its length and with the type of material. All-fiberglass paddles usually run about 3 to 3½ pounds; all-wood paddles, about 2½ to 3½ pounds, and a little heavier if the wood is oak or spruce. Composites, paddles made of several materials, may run from 3 to 4 pounds. Paddle weight is not a big factor in cruising. In racing it becomes a bigger factor.

The shafts of canoe paddles vary in diameter. Some manufacturers "oval" them—make them elliptical—in order to combat twisting in the canoeist's hand and to help the canoeist to identify "blade orientation" when preparing to execute the "roll."

In wintertime, shafts of metal, such as aluminum, are colder to the user's hands than are shafts of other materials. Metal, however, does have good strength advantages.

What type of grip, if any, to have at the top of the shaft is a personal decision, best determined by testing.

The width of the scoop, or blade, is very important. For the average, weekend-only cruiser, a scoop width of 8 to 10 inches, not more, and a scoop length of 14 to 18 inches are about right. These dimensions give good surface area to move, steer, and control the canoe. They will allow for some "slippage"— which means, not actual slippage, but reduced resistance.

Water is a fluid, yes. But in paddling it is best thought of as a solid mass that offers resistance. If the paddler only *pulls* with his or her lower arm, the canoe will move the distance of the pull and no more. But if he or she also *pushes* the top of the shaft with the other arm, and uses his or her body and not just the arm muscles for the effort, torque will be developed and the boat will be given velocity. The motion is somewhat like that of a pole vaulter. He runs down his track, plants his pole, and swings his body up and over the bar. So with the paddler. He plants the paddle in the water and swings or pushes himself and the boat past a point.

Kayak Paddles

Paddles for kayaks are more complex than canoe paddles—in both construction and use.

Kayak paddles have two types of blades. The slalom type has square tips at the ends like a canoe paddle. It puts the maximum surface into the water and is ideal for whitewater cruising. The downriver type has rounded tips and will enter and leave the water with minimum resistance.

When you have decided on the material and the type of tip of your kayak paddle, you have a third choice to make. Will your kayak paddle be for "no control hand"? For "left-hand control"? For "right-hand control"?

All kayak paddles are double-enders. Unlike canoe paddles, which have only one scoop, kayak paddles have a scoop at each end.

For the type of kayak paddle which has no control hand, the scoops (blades) are parallel to each other. You just put them in the water and go to work. The drawback with these is that the end which is up and out of the water is broadside to the wind. Thus, a headwind can slow you down, and a tailwind in a stiff blow will tend to pull the blade out of your hand or to bowl you over.

A kayak paddle with left-hand control or right-hand control has its scoop set at a 90-degree angle to the scoop on the other end. Thus the end that is up and in the air presents its edge, not its broad side, to the wind.

With left-hand control, at the end of the left-side stroke the kayaker rotates the shaft with the left hand so that the left scoop comes up with its edge to the wind and the right scoop is presented correctly to the water. As the stroke on the right side is ended, the left scoop is ready for the water without twisting the shaft.

The kayak paddle with right-hand control functions in just the opposite way—that is, the shaft is twisted with the right hand only.

Which type you choose is not dependent on whether you are left-handed or right-handed. Left- or right-handedness seems to have little or no bearing on the choice. What is important is that when you have become accustomed to a control blade for one side or the other, you stay with it. It is very difficult—a feat requiring a lot of concentration—to switch between left-hand and right-hand types. For that reason, it is desirable to buy two kayak paddles of the type you choose. Thus, if a paddle is broken or swept away in the water, you will have a spare of the correct type.

The kayak paddle, whatever the type, is an efficient means of propelling the craft. It does not have to be switched from one hand to the other or from one side of the boat to the other. However, it can be a nuisance when you are maneuvering in a tight area or when the end that is up in the air catches in low, overhanging trees.

The length of the kayak paddle depends on the physical attributes of the user. For racing kayakers who are in good condition and operate from a standard seated position in standard-design boats, the proper paddle length is determined by standing the paddle with one blade on the floor and extending an arm fully out, above head level, and wrapping the fingers over the blade in the air.

For the average user, the length is adequate if the paddle blade that is in the air comes up to the base of the extended hand. If the paddle is shorter, the user (even though he did not experience discomfort initially) will gradually come to feel uncomfortable and to find it difficult to exert control. He will also come to feel that his effort is wasted in part, and that it is not giving him the propulsion it should.

The blade width of most kayak paddles is from 8 to 12 inches, and the blade length is about 14 inches. A length of about 14 inches, with a width of 8 to 10 inches, is best for the average user. It will get good resistance in the water and yet not be unduly fatiguing.

The weight of kayak paddles, like that of canoe paddles, is determined by their length and their composition. A superlight racing paddle weighs about 2 1/4 pounds. A paddle built of fiberglass and aluminum weighs about 3 to 5 pounds.

Kayak paddles are made of various materials. There are all-wood types in which the shaft and blades consist of laminated strips, or in which a laminated shaft is joined to molded blades. There are types with blades of six to eight layers of fiberglass, joined to either a fiberglass or an aluminum shaft. There are kayak paddles made of wood sandwiched between layers of fiberglass and kayak paddles made of foam compositions wrapped in fiberglass. Those with fiberglass blades and aluminum shafts usually come with a rounded shaft. On paddles for left-hand control or right-hand control, there is a loss of advantage, especially for the beginner, because they do not have the oval shape that comes to tell the user when the paddle is in the correct position.

Shafts come in varying diameters. The "feel" of the shaft is highly important because it has a great deal to do with how natural and comfortable the paddle seems when in use.

Poles

In the early years of the United States, fur traders used poles to propel their rafts and their canoes up and down rivers to fur-trading posts. Then they found that the Indians, whom they were frequently trying to elude, moved faster by using paddles. So they adopted the Indians' method, and poles disappeared.

In recent years poles have made a comeback, in part because of the availability of improved materials. Poles of fiberglass or aluminum that are eight to ten feet long weigh four to six pounds at most. Wooden poles may range up to about ten pounds.

Poles are used for canoes but not for kayaks.

One advantage of poling is that the canoeist stands while propelling his craft. Thus he sees much farther than the canoeist who is seated or kneeling, and he gets much earlier warning of logs, rocks, dams, and other obstacles that lie ahead.

One disadvantage of poling is that there are few pole manufacturers. A second is that a deep lake or a river channel will sometimes be beyond the reach of a pole to bottom. However, even though poles are round, they can be used as kayak paddles, since the surface area of the section of pole in the water approaches that of the kayak paddle.

A manufactured pole is relatively expensive, though not much more so than some kayak paddles.

Sails

Sails are yet another means of canoe propulsion. Canoe sailing did not originate with the American Indians. It originated in England and among the fur traders around the Great Lakes.

Today, most major canoe manufacturers offer sailing rigs for their boats. The equipment includes an aluminum mast and sometimes a boom; a set of leeboards (two dagger-shaped boards to hang over the side and give the canoe a keel so that it will run straight); and a Dacron sail containing about 55 to 65 square feet of sail area.

Canoe sailing is now done widely for pleasure. In fact, it has progressed to a point at which canoe sailing races are being conducted.

In a brisk wind, canoes under sail will probably outrun most other sailboats and also paddled kayaks. The craft are very fast, and sailing them is great fun.

The rigs retail from about $85 to $150, depending on the type of equipment, the number of accessories, and the manufacturer.

Rowing

Canoe rowing has been popular in Europe for a long time, and it is beginning to win acceptance in this country. There are now three or four manufacturers of complete rowing rigs—slide seats, riggers, and sweeps.

The slide seats go back as the rower pulls and draws up his legs. In one type the seat moves on rollers. In another type a greased strip moves in a slot. The former type is best.

The riggers of rowing canoes are equivalent to oarlocks, but they are different from standard oarlocks and look like the riggers on rowing shells. They are often formed from a lightweight metal tubing, such as aluminum.

The sweeps are the equivalent of oars. They average six to eight feet in length and may be as long as ten feet. They are so named because the way the boat moves makes them appear to sweep through the water in an arc. Sweeps are now made only in wood.

The cost of a rowing rig can easily exceed that of the canoe itself.

If you adhere to the traditionalist view of the canoe as something to be paddled by one or two persons, then rowing seems to defeat the purpose.

The rowing rig has its limits. It is best for open bodies of water; it is not suited for closed or narrow rivers.

Outboard Motors

Outboard motors have been hooked onto canoes ever since the outboard motor was invented. Since a canoe's configuration is an efficient one, it is propelled rapidly by even a motor of low horsepower—which is the only type that should be used. A motor of five to seven horsepower will send a canoe through the water at about ten to twelve miles an hour.

Square-sterned canoes were built to take motors. However, transoms for side mounting on conventional canoes can be bought and easily installed.

In our opinion, again, a gasoline-driven motor seems to defeat the purpose of canoeing—namely, to go quietly into some hitherto unseen area and to get good exercise with a paddle without disturbing the peace and the wildlife.

Maybe the motored canoe is all right for limited uses—for handicapped people or for people in poor physical condition, or in situations where long runs have to be made to bring perishable food back to camp during hot weather.

There is another alternative to paddling—the electric outboard motor. It is small and light and will operate off a battery for about two to three hours before a recharge is needed. And, of course, there are no fumes and no noise.

Following is a listing of selected manufacturers of canoe and kayak propulsion equipment, with descriptions of their products.

As with our earlier canoe and kayak listing, the prices given for Canadian manufacturers will normally be in Canadian dollars. Some Canadian manufacturers include U.S. import duties and taxes in their prices. Where they do not, the gain from the current favorable exchange rate can be affected. In dealing with a Canadian firm, the prospective U.S. buyer's best bet might be to ask for a delivered price expressed in U.S. dollars.

In this chapter the authors have attempted to include, primarily, actual manufacturers (not just vendors) of paddles for canoes and kayaks. Nearly all canoe and kayak manufacturers also sell paddles—whether they make the paddles themselves or buy the paddles elsewhere.

Some of the companies listed may manufacture part of their paddle lines and purchase the rest.

In any case, paddles are offered by boat companies that are *not listed* in this chapter. These companies may offer very good paddles (in some cases these may be paddles produced by the manufacturers listed here) and at very competitive prices.

AMERICAN FIBER-LITE, INC.
PO Box 67
Marion, Illinois 62959
Phone: (618) 997-5474

American Fiber-Lite offers canoe paddles and kayak blades constructed with a plastic paddle section and an aluminum shaft. They come in lengths of 4½ feet, 5 feet, and 5½ feet, and they are priced at $15.

BART HAUTHAWAY
640 Boston Post Road
Weston, Massachusetts 02193
Phone: (617) 894-1027

Bart Hauthaway offers both canoe and kayak paddles. The canoe paddle is constructed of a pressure-molded, white fiberglass blade with red trim at the throat, a straight-grained fir shaft, and a T-grip. All wood is finished with three coats of urethane varnish. The blade area is 7¾ inches by 23 inches. Lengths range from 56 inches to 68 inches. The price is $24.

The kayak paddles are constructed of pressure-molded, white fiberglass scoops, feathered at 90 degrees, with a red trim at the throat, and a one-piece fir shaft. The wood is finished with three coats of urethane varnish. Spoons are available for right- or left-hand control. Models include the Spoon Blade, the MiniSpoon Blade, the Junior Spoon Blade, the Flat Blade, and the Junior Flat Blade. The prices range from $30 to $35.

BLUE HOLE CANOE COMPANY
Sunbright, Tennessee 37872
Phone: (615) 628-2116

Blue Hole Canoe Company offers a lightweight canoe paddle constructed with a neoprene-covered (6061-T6) shaft; a solid, injection-molded plastic T-grip handle; and an extruded ABS blade. The standard blade dimensions are 8 inches wide by 25 inches long.

This paddle is available in standard lengths ranging from 54 to 66 inches (in two-inch increments), with other lengths available on special order. The paddle weighs about 2¾ pounds. The price is $38.

CANNON PRODUCTS, INC.
2345 Northwest Eighth Avenue—PO Box 835
Faribault, Minnesota 55021
Phone: (507) 334-4331

Cannon builds paddles and oars for canoes, kayaks, boats, and inflatables. All in all, it constructs 18 different models of paddles and oars with an ABS polymer grip and blade and an aluminum shaft or with a wooden shaft and grip and an ABS blade. All of the blades are filled with a foam flotation core which prevents them from sinking when they are dropped into the water. The blades of canoe paddles are 6¾, 7, 8, and 9 inches wide, and the blades of kayak paddles are 6¾ and 8 inches wide. The kayak paddles are available with a one-piece shaft or with a two-piece shaft with a snap-lock joint. The oars come with a hardwood shaft and an ABS polymer blade.

Cannon's canoe paddles range in length from 4½ feet to 5½ feet. Its kayak paddles range from 6 feet 11 inches to 9 feet.

CARLISLE AuSABLE PADDLE
COMPANY
4562 North Down River Road—PO Box 150
Grayling, Michigan 49738
Phone: (517) 348-9886

Carlisle AuSable Paddle Company builds canoe paddles, kayak paddles, and boat oars with ABS plastic blades and aluminum shafts (two weights—a standard and a "heavy duty" 6061-T6), with canoe paddles offering an ABS pear or T-grip. The aluminum shafts are covered with plastic for comfort. The canoe paddles range in length from three feet to six feet, with the blades 8 inches wide and 20 inches long. The kayak paddles range in length from six feet to nine feet, and also have blades that are 8 by 20 inches. The kayak paddles (breakdown models) also feature an ac-

cessory conversion kit—two canoe-type shafts and grips that are used to convert one kayak paddle to two canoe paddles.

The boat oars have the same construction as the paddles, except that the blades are 5½ inches wide by 26 inches long. However, oars with blades of 8 by 20 inches are also available.

Standard canoe paddles range in cost, by length, from $10.25 to $12.65; heavy-duty paddles, from $13.55 to $15.35; extra-heavy-duty paddles, from $18.10 to $19.75; standard paddles with T-grip, from $12.95 to $14.15; and heavy-duty paddles with T-grip, from $15.05 to $16.85.

Standard kayak paddles cost from $19.95 to $21.55; heavy-duty paddles, from $23.70 to $26.30; standard breakdown paddles, from $24.65 to $25.95; and heavy-duty breakdown paddles, from $28.40 to $30.80.

Oars come in a wide selection that includes standard and breakdown models and heavy duty and extra-heavy-duty rafting models. These oars range in price from $16.25 to above $60.

CAVINESS WOODWORKING
COMPANY, INC.
PO Box 710
Calhoun City, Mississippi 38916
Phone: (601) 628-5195

Feather Brand paddles and oars, by Caviness, come in various models including "superlight" ones, with oak inserts in high-stress areas. The blades vary from 6½ to 8 inches in width and from "beavertail" designs to a flat-tip one with the shaft tapered down about two-thirds of the length. The laminated wood construction of the oars is similar to that of the paddles.

CHESTNUT CANOE COMPANY, LTD.
PO Box 185
Oromocto, New Brunswick, Canada
E2V 2G5
Phone: (506) 357-3338

Chestnut Canoe Company offers a line of wood canoe paddles to go with its many canoes. The blades are offered in widths of 6 and 8 inches, and there is also a tapered blade which is 5¼ inches wide at the shaft and 4¾ inches wide at the tip. All of the paddles are available in three-inch increments from 4 feet 3 inches long to 5 feet 9 inches long.

The prices, in Canadian dollars, range from $12 to $16.33.

COLEMAN COMPANY, INC.
PO Box 1762
Wichita, Kansas 67201

Coleman offers three models of wood canoe paddles—all are of spruce coated with urethane varnish, and all have 7-inch-wide blades. The Stinger is a five-lamination model of Canadian white spruce in 54- and 60-inch lengths. The Trader is a seven-lamination model of Canadian white spruce in lengths of 54, 60, and 64 inches. The Sugar Island is a nine-lamination model of Sitka spruce in lengths of 54 and 60 inches.

The prices are $8 for the Stinger, $18 for the Trader, and $28 for the Sugar Island.

EDDYLINE NORTHWEST, LTD.
8423 Mukilteo Speedway
Everett, Washington 98204
Phone: (206) 743-9252

Eddyline offers two models of kayak blades, the Eddyline Flat and the Eddyline Spoon. Both models are constructed of epoxy and S-glass spoons with aluminum shafts (thermally insulated) and ovaled hand grips.

The Eddyline Flat, an all-purpose paddle designed for river or ocean touring, has just a slight spoon.

The Eddyline Spoon has a lot of longitudinal curvature and very little lateral curvature, giving this blade plenty of "push power." This type of blade is excellent for the "heavy" river paddler who needs good power, but the blade could prove quite tiring for the average "Sunday cruiser."

GREAT CANADIAN CANOE
45 Water Street
Worcester, Massachusetts 01604
Phone: (617) 755-5237

Great Canadian offers the paddles for its canoe and kayak lines. The buyer can choose from canoe and kayak paddles made of wood and of plastic blades and aluminum shafts.

The wooden canoe paddles come in three models.

The Maine Guide paddle is constructed of northern ash, with a blade 7 inches wide and a mushroom-type grip. The lengths are 54, 57, 60, 63, and 66 inches. The price is approximately $15.

The J-stroke paddle is constructed of laminated mahoganies and is designed to minimize or eliminate the J-stroke by fitting the wide portion of the blade under the curvature of the canoe. The lengths are 57, 60, and 63 inches. The prices range from about $18 to about $20.

The "economy" paddle is designed for occasional paddling. It is made of two pieces of spruce and, at about $5, is quite inexpensive. The lengths are 65 and 60 inches.

The aluminum shaft/plastic paddles have aluminum shafts and ABS plastic blades and grips. The blade dimensions are 8 by 18 inches, and the total paddle lengths are 54, 60, and 66 inches. The price is about $8.

The aluminum and plastic kayak blades come in two types, one with a straight (flat) blade for use with canoes and the other with a curved blade. The length is eight feet, and the prices for the two types are about $21 and $22, respectively.

GRUMMAN BOATS
Marathon, New York 13803
Phone: (607) 849-3211

Grumman Boats produces, along with its canoes, a line of wooden paddles and a line of paddles that is made in part of ABS plastic.

The wooden paddle, referred to as the T-Grip, is constructed of Sitka spruce and cedar laminates, with a hardwood spline at the tip. The blade width is 7 inches, and the blade lengths are 56, 60, and 62 inches.

The partly plastic paddles, called the Masterlites, have an eight-inch-wide ABS blade that is joined by a shaft of hollow, anodized aluminum to a plastic, mushroom-type hand-grip. The lengths are 4½ feet, 5 feet, 5½ feet, and 6 feet.

The T-Grip, in spruce or cedar, sells for $28, and the Masterlite for $11.25.

ILIAD, INC.
55 Washington Street
Norwell, Massachusetts 02061
Phone: (617) 878-3404

Iliad builds two types or models of canoe and kayak paddles, the Wildwater and the Vagabond.

The Wildwater paddles are constructed with high-density fiberglass cloth and epoxy, pressure-molded onto an aluminum, ovaled shaft which is covered with an extruded neoprene tube. The canoe paddle's grip is also pressure-molded around the shaft, thus reducing the likelihood of its loosening or breaking. The shaft extends to within three inches of the blade tip and to within about one-half inch of the top of the canoe-paddle grip.

The canoe-paddle blades have areas of 22 × 8¾ inches, 25 × 9 inches, 28 × 9¼ inches, and 22 × 8⅜ inches (a spooned blade). The lengths are 51 through 72 inches in three-inch increments.

The kayak blades are 22 × 8⅜ inches for the spooned model and 22 × 8¾ inches for the flat model. The lengths are 78 through 88 inches in two-inch increments.

The Vagabond paddles are designed for the recreational paddler. Hence, they are constructed somewhat differently from the Whitewater models, and with less expensive materials. Polyester resin and roving, rather than epoxy and fiberglass cloth, are used in the blades of the Vagabond paddles. Also, only one blade size is offered (22 × 8⅝ inches). However, these paddles and blades will meet all the requirements of the average paddler.

The canoe-type Wildwater paddles are priced at $43, and the kayak type at $65. The canoe-type Vagabond models are priced at $27, and the kayak type at $39.50.

A. C. MACKENZIE RIVER COMPANY
PO Box 9301
Richmond Heights, Missouri 63117
Phone: (1-314) 781-7221

The A. C. Mackenzie River Company is the home of the Sylvester pole. This pole is constructed of lightweight aircraft aluminum, weighs only 2.5 pounds, is 12 feet long, is easily and quickly dismantled for carrying or storage, and will float if dropped into the water. It was developed by past national poling cham-

Brothers Syl Beletz (left) and Al Beletz show off their championship Sylvester poles.

pion Syl Beletz after many years of experimenting with wood, fiberglass, and aluminum. An interesting fact to note is that there is no record of a Sylvester pole ever breaking, either in cruising or during competition. For those of you who have never heard of or tried poling, brothers Al, Syl, and Frank Beletz have written a very good book on the subject, *Canoe Poling*, which is available from the Mackenzie company (see Appendix).

MID-CANADA FIBERGLASS, LTD.
Box 1599
New Liskeard, Ontario, Canada P0J 1P0
Phone: (705) 647-6549

Mid-Canada, maker of the Scott canoe line, also offers a line of one-piece wooden paddles in ash and birch. These are called the Teal paddles. Their dimensions (in inches), and their prices (in Canadian funds) are: 5 × 54, $12.95; 5 × 60, $13.95; 6 × 60, $15.95, and 8 × 60, $22.95.

NORSE PADDLE COMPANY
PO Box 77
Pine Grove Mills, Pennsylvania 16868
Phone: (814) 237-7504

Norse Paddle Company makes both canoe and kayak paddles, and does a really good job of it. Norse paddles are built of pressure-molded epoxy/fiberglass cloth and have fiberglass-covered aluminum shafts. All blades have a piece of aluminum molded into the tip for abrasion resistance.

The T-grips of the canoe paddles are made of molded fiberglass. The canoe paddles have 7½-inch-wide blades and are available in lengths ranging from 53 inches to 69 inches in one-inch increments.

The blades of the kayak paddles are feathered at 90 degrees. The standard kayak blade width is 7¾ inches, and the kayak paddle lengths are 78, 81, 83, 84, and 87 inches.

All Norse paddles float horizontally when dropped in water.

The prices are $44 for the canoe paddle, $60 for the kayak flat blade, and $62 for the kayak spoon blade.

OLD TOWN CANOE COMPANY
Box 5481
Old Town, Maine 04468
Phone (207) 827-5513

Old Town Canoe Company offers canoe paddles in solid spruce, maple, and ash and in laminated wood. It also offers a fiberglass whitewater paddle.

Wooden paddles are available in lengths of from four to six feet in three-inch increments. Maine Guide styles are available in lengths of from five to six feet in three-inch increments.

Kayak paddles are constructed of two pressure-molded white fiberglass blades that are feathered at 90 degrees on a yellow fiberglass shaft. Both spoon and flat blades are available. The lengths are 76, 78, 80, 82, and 84 inches.

Also available is an oar which is constructed in the same way as the kayak paddle (except that it has only one spoon). It comes in a seven-foot length and is priced at $120.

The prices of the canoe paddles are:

Paddle, single, spruce, ash, or maple, with 6½-inch blade
    In ash or maple $28
    In spruce $30
Paddle, single, spruce, ash, or maple, with 7¾-inch blade
    In ash or maple $29
    In spruce $32
Paddle, single, Maine Guide, maple or ash, with 7¾-inch blade $38
Paddle, single, laminated, 7¾-inch blade $26
Paddle, No. 2 grade, any wood $24
Whitewater paddle, single, fiberglass blade with T-grip (52, 56, 58, 60, 62, 64, 66, and 68 inches) $48

The prices of the kayak paddles are:

Spoon-blade double paddle (76, 78, 80, 82, and 84 inches) $58
Spoon-blade double paddle, 96 inches, with drip rings $60
Flat-blade double paddle (76, 78, 80, 82, and 84 inches) $56
Flat-blade double paddle, 96 inches, with drip rings $58

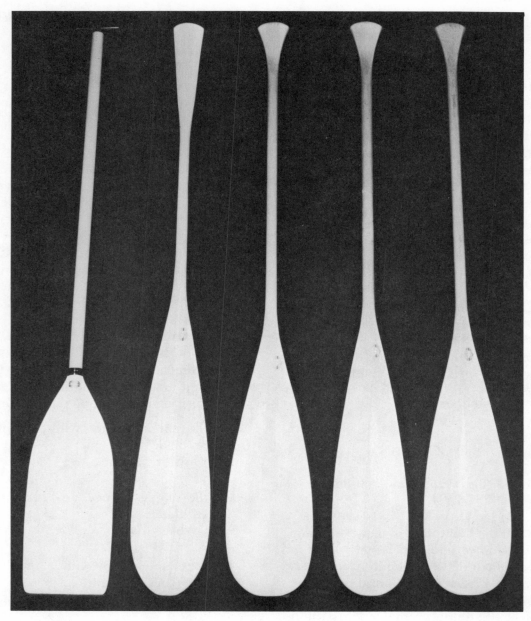

Five canoe paddles by Old Town. From left: Whitewater paddle, fiberglass blade; Main Guide model, maple or ash, 7¾-inch blade; laminated, 7¾-inch blade; spruce, ash, or maple, 6½-inch blade; spruce, ash, or maple, 7¾-inch blade.

PERCEPTION, INC.
Box 64
Liberty, South Carolina 29657
Phone: (803) 859-7518

Perception offers paddles for both canoes and kayaks. Pressure-molded epoxy/fiberglass blades are joined to aluminum shafts. The canoe paddles have an epoxy grip.

The tips of the blades are of inlaid aluminum molded in, with rivets at each corner. The shafts of kayak paddles are ovaled for comfort and orientation.

Also available, for competition, are light-weight paddles of graphite/Kevlar.

The standard lengths are 56 to 64 inches for canoe paddles, and 78 to 85 inches for kayak paddles.

The prices (rounded) are: canoe paddle, $32; graphite/Kevlar canoe paddle, $50; flat-blade kayak paddle, $52; spoon-blade kayak paddle, $52; and graphite/Kevlar kayak paddle, $77.

RAINBOW PADDLE
PO Box 9213
San Jose, California 95157

Rainbow Paddle offers a lightweight, extremely strong kayak paddle that is constructed of epoxy resin and fiberglass cloth and has a vaulting-pole shaft. This paddle was under development by Tom Johnson (U.S. Olympic whitewater team coach, 1972) for several years. It can be used for flat-water (Olympic) and whitewater racing as well as for cruising and surfing.

If you want to purchase one paddle that will meet all your needs (at a reasonable price), you should certainly look at this one. The price is about $60.

SAWYER WOODWORKING
8891 Rogue River Highway
Rogue River, Oregon 97537
Phone: (503) 582-1350

Says the company:
"Handcrafted, lightweight and extra strong, Sawyer's paddles number the largest combination of paddles available in the country. (Would you believe a total of over 1,500 possible combinations?)"

Construction starts with a straight-grained, full-round dowel for a shaft. Then the grips are added. The blades are cut from laminated blocks of assorted woods and are fitted and reinforced with a minimum of two layers of fiberglass cloth. The entire paddle then gets two coats of spar varnish.

Also available are paddles with fiberglass tips.

The canoe paddles include:

SCT-8: Laminated blade, T-grip; vertical-grain oval shaft; 8-inch × 20-inch fiberglass-reinforced blade with two layers on each side in the tip area. Lengths, 54 and 60 inches. Price, $14.

SC-8: Laminated grip and blade; vertical-grain oval shaft; 8-inch × 23-inch fiberglass-reinforced blade with two layers on each side in the tip area. Lengths, 50, 52, 54, 56, 58, and 60 inches. Price, $18.50.

SC-10: Same as SC-8 but with 10-inch × 23-inch blade. Price, $20.

B-10: Laminated grip and blade; full-round vertical-grain shaft; 10-inch × 23-inch fiberglass-reinforced blade with two layers on each side in the tip area. Lengths, 50, 52, 54, 56, 58, and 60 inches. Price, $25.

B-10: Same model as above but with optional angle blade and custom inlay. Price, $25.

B-12: Laminated grip and blade; full-round vertical-grain shaft; 12-inch × 23-inch fiberglass-reinforced blade with three layers on each side in the tip area. Lengths, 50, 52, 54, 56, 58, and 60 inches. Price, $27.

C-8: Laminated grip and blades; full-round vertical-grain shaft; 8-inch × 23-inch fiberglass-reinforced blade with two layers on each side in the tip area. Lengths, 50, 52, 54, 56, 58, 60, 63, 66, and 69 inches. Price, $23.50.

S-8: T-grip and two-piece blade; full-round vertical-grain shaft; 8-inch × 23-inch fiberglass-reinforced blade with two layers on each side in the tip area. Lengths, 50, 52, 54, 56, 58, 60, 63, 66, and 69 inches.

WW-9: T-grip with laminated 9-inch × 23-inch blade; full-round vertical-grain shaft; two full layers of fiberglass on each side of blade. Model features optional fiberglass inlay shaft reinforcement and optional solid fiberglass tip. Lengths, 50, 52, 54, 56, 58, 60, 63, 66, and 69 inches.

SEDA PRODUCTS
PO Box 997
Chula Vista, California 92010
Phone: (714) 425-3222

Seda manufactures a wooden and a fiberglass canoe paddle and an all-fiberglass kayak paddle.

The wooden canoe paddle is made from 11 pieces of aged spruce, mahogany, and maple, laminated together and finished with three coats of ultra spar marine varnish. A stainless steel hammering protects the blade tip. The blade area is 7½ inches by 22 inches. The paddle lengths are 58, 60, 62, 64, and 66 inches.

The fiberglass and epoxy canoe paddle uses a vaulting-pole shaft with either a polyester/fiberglass or an epoxy/fiberglass blade and grip. A stainless steel hammering protects the tip on both types of construction. The paddle lengths are 58, 60, 62, 64, and 66 inches.

The kayak paddle is constructed of a fiberglass blade molded onto an epoxy/fiberglass vaulting-pole shaft. The blades are made from compression-molded and reinforced plastic, consisting of woven cloth and polyester or epoxy resin (depending on the order), with a stainless steel hammering on the tips. The shaft extends approximately two-thirds of the way down into the blade's length, giving the whole assembly good strength and rigidity. The paddle blades are straight or are feathered at 90 degrees. The paddle lengths are 80, 82, and 84 inches.

6

Flotation Gear and Helmets

There is a cardinal axiom in paddling that everyone—novice or expert—should remember. The axiom is: "Boats don't cause accidents—people do!" If you leave your life jacket in your car or have it stuffed down in your boat, it won't help you at all if you make a mistake and take an unplanned swim. The same applies to helmets, though here there is another axiom that says: "The shallower the water, the more necessary the helmet."

Under provisions of the Federal Boat Safety Act of 1971, life jackets or PFD's (personal flotation devices) are required equipment on all recreational boats. They are also required to be aboard by the game and wildlife commissions (whose agents are game and fish wardens) of almost all the states. In addition, on some rivers the actual wearing of PFD's is required because of hazardous conditions.

PFD's fall into five categories that are approved by the U.S. Coast Guard. Of these, four are now approved for use on all recrea-

tional-type boats. The fifth is more specialized.

Type I PFD's are designed to turn an unconscious person in the water from a facedown position to a position that is vertical or slightly backward. A PFD of this type must have in excess of 20 pounds of positive buoyancy. It can have rigid or flexible foam that is covered with canvas or kapok, held in heavy plastic envelopes inside an outer covering of canvas.

Type II PFD's are designed to turn an unconscious person in the water from a facedown position to a position that is slightly backward or vertical. Positive buoyancy must be at least 15½ pounds. This is the least expensive and the most common type of life jacket. A PFD of this type is quite adequate on small rivers and lakes, but because of its construction it is not recommended for use where the person in the water might encounter rocks or other such obstacles. This is because most jackets of this type have plastic envelopes which can easily be damaged—thus admitting water and changing the jacket from a flotation device to an anchor.

Type III PFD's are designed to keep a conscious person in a vertical or a slightly backward position. A PFD of this type must have at least 15 pounds of positive buoyancy. Life jackets in this category usually have a foam core inside a nylon cover and are designed to be worn much as a suit vest would be. Their design permits a greater amount of movement, both in and out of water, than does either a Type I or a Type II, PFD. PFD's of this type must be worn by all whitewater competitors. They are generally lightweight, and they range in cost from $18 to $36.

Type IV PFD's are designed for throwing to a person in the water and not for wearing. Their buoyancy must be at least 16.5 pounds. PFD's in this category are usually buoyant cushions (sometimes mistakenly used as seat cushions and "life rings").

Type V PFD's are special-purpose devices which are available in two types. One is the Mae West vest design, which uses carbon dioxide. Aircraft pilots use it on flights over water. The other type is very bulky, but it provides an extraordinary amount of flotation. It is worn by rafters, ferryboat pilots, and others.

Readers should note that the so-called ski belts are not acceptable as PFD's. One reason is that, worn at the midpoint of the body, they are as likely to hold a person head down in the water as they are to hold him legs down. The other reason is that most ski belts are not sufficiently rugged in construction to take much abrasion.

Helmets—to wear or not to wear?

For an average, weekend, flat-water cruiser, the question of whether to have or wear a helmet is not a problem. The answer, quite simply, is: It is not necessary unless you are going into whitewater. If you are going into light whitewater in which rocks are present, a helmet should be worn. If you are going into heavy whitewater, a helmet is a must.

For the paddler who goes into wild water all the time (or even most of the time), a helmet is as necessary as a paddle and a life jacket.

(You might even say that it is the head's life jacket.)

Helmets come in many shapes, sizes, and types of construction. Until recently, the only lightweight helmets available to the paddler were webbed leather or plastic hockey and bicycle helmets. Today there are helmets made of high-impact plastic, still used mainly as hockey helmets, and full-blown fiberglass helmets that are designed for canoe racing.

Following is a listing of some major manufacturers of life jackets and helmets, with descriptions of their products. In some cases, information is provided on where these products may be inspected and bought.

GENTEX CORPORATION
Carbondale, Pennsylvania 18407
Phone: (717) 282-3550

Gentex manufactures nothing but life vests—vests for sailors, vests for fishermen, vests for hunters, and vests for water skiers. Where are the vests for canoeists? Answer: All of these vests can be used by canoeists. Some are better than others, but in general the paddler can just choose the model he likes and feel assured that it will protect him.

This statement must be qualified in the case of the whitewater paddler, who should consider only a model with a zipper and a belt or belts. Why? Because in whitewater the swimmer must not only stay afloat but must also cope with swirls, holes, and the possibility of being thrown against rocks. All of these hazards tend to remove any vest that is not well secured.

All of the Gentex vests are constructed with two or more PVC foam panels with nylon outer shells, an inner lining, and adjustable side panels. The Rainbow, Blue Horizon, Crew, and Youth vests come with front zippers only. The Sport and Sailor's vests come with a front zipper and a belt around the waist. The Competition Ski vest and the Tri-Color Ski vest come with two belts only.

The prices range from $27.50 for the Youth vest to $42.50 for the Sailing and Blue Horizon models.

Gentex (above) says its Youth vest is more than just "a miniature adult vest." It is designed to encourage children to wear PFD's. It has a high waist for free movement, front flaps to make sitting comfortable, and a cover of colorful patchwork nylon.

Medalist's Recreational Vest (above) has full-rotation arm openings, is built of closed-cell marine foam and nylon, and has a full-length zipper.

(Below, left) Specially designed for the duck hunter is this life vest by Gentex. It is in camouflage design, and its narrow lapels are designed to allow comfortable shouldering of a shotgun.

MEDALIST WATER SPORTS
11525 Sorrento Valley Road
San Diego, California 92121
Phone: (714) 453-1141
Toll-free order number: (800) 854-2672
   (except California)

Medalist's Cut'nJump line includes the Buoyant Vest, a Type II PFD with three pads—two front and one shoulder—of polyethylene foam covered with a nylon shell and held on the wearer by a tie string at the top and a web belt and a snap catch at the waist. Cost, $5.95.

The Boating Vest consists of two front and two rear polyethylene foam panels which are connected at the shoulders by a nylon outer jacket and under the arms by nylon lacing.

The vest has a zipper only in front. Price, $9.75.

The Recreational Vest is essentially a one-piece polyethylene foam panel with a nylon outer shell and a full-length zipper. This vest has full-rotation arm openings. A model with pockets in the front for shells is available for hunters. Cost, $12.95 and $13.95.

The Ski Vest consists of two front, two side, and two rear polyethylene foam panels with a nylon outer shell and two belts. Cost. $14.50.

The Sailing Vest is the Medalist PFD that is most suitable for use by the whitewater paddler. At $14.50 it is also a good buy for the average paddler. It has front and rear panels of polyethylene foam, a nylon outer shell, an "apron," a waist belt, and a full-length zipper.

The company also makes water skis and accessories and wet suits.

SEDA PRODUCTS
PO Box 997
Chula Vista, California 92010
Phone: (714) 425-3222

Seda life vests are rated USCG Class III. These life vests are constructed of narrow polyethylene tubes (more than 100 in each jacket) which are sewn into a nylon envelope. The envelope is constructed from double-ply nylon taffeta. All seams are double-stitched with heavy-duty Dacron thread.

Metal zippers of the same type that is used on wet suits are used on all vests. The lower part of the vest is designed to be easily turned up for use in kayaks.

This is an excellent vest for paddlers who like to run big whitewater. Its ability to do the job is demonstrated by the fact that it is the most popular vest among the top 50 U.S. whitewater paddlers.

Price, $33. Available at most canoe centers as well as from the company.

Seda offers four helmets for canoeists and kayakers. As described by the company, they are "fiberglass long style, heavy duty covering ears; fiberglass short style, heavy duty above ears; lightweight nylon, racing medium duty protection; lightweight polycarbon, translu-

cent blue, medium duty." The prices of these helmets, respectively, are $27, $27, $15, and $16.

The fiberglass helmets are of hand-laid fiberglass constructed of a high-impact resin. Since the inner padding does not absorb water, the helmet will float. Space has been left between the padding so that customers who prefer drainage/ventilation holes can drill in their own. The chin straps are of tubular nylon webbing.

The lightest helmet has been designed especially for wear in whitewater canoeing. Its shell is of injection-molded high-impact nylon with narrow drainage slots. It weighs about 13 ounces.

Seda also makes wet suits, cartop carriers, and a lot of other paddling accessories.

STEARNS MANUFACTURING COMPANY
PO Box 1498
St. Cloud, Minnesota 56301
Phone: (612) 252-1642

Stearns is a manufacturer of PFD's, foul-weather gear, and other types of protective gear for the paddler, the sailor, the water-skier, and so on. Stearns PFD's are constructed of a closed-cell PVC foam around which is wrapped an outer shell of nylon, cotton-polyester denim, or polyester, depending on the model. These PFD's are fastened by a heavy-duty body strap and rustproofed zippers of metal or Vislon. The inside of the vest has a nylon mesh lining.

The PFD line for canoeing, kayaking, and rafting includes the Deliverance model, which features a urethane-coated nylon outer shell and lining, and wide PVC tubes all around. A separate set of tubes in the lower section constitutes an apron that can be worn up or down, permitting the jacket to be used in kayaking. The Deliverance has a waist tie and a zipper. The price is $35.80.

The Whitewater River Rafting Vest has PVC panels covered with a urethane-coated nylon outer shell and lining, a flotation collar, and a belted apron, plus two upper-body belts. The price is $51.35.

Pee Wee are priced at $21.20, and the Kindergaard is priced at $23.80.

WILDWATER DESIGNS KITS
Penllyn, Pennsylvania 19422

Wildwater Designs, whose owner Charlie Walbridge is himself a first-rate paddler, was created to make the best equipment available to all paddlers in kit form at the lowest price possible. Charlie has been at this for five years as a business, and he spent six to eight years before that just trying to come up with all the unusual equipment needed by a big paddler (he is about 6 feet 4) as well as the equipment needed by an average paddler.

This effort has produced the High Flotation Life Vest Kit. Although the kit is not Coast Guard–approved (the Coast Guard will not approve kits), it far exceeds the USCG requirements and the International Canoe Federation's even more stringent requirements for racing PFD's.

Wildwater vests are constructed of wide and thick PVC foam tubes enclosed in a 3 1/2-ounce coated nylon packcloth shell and closed with a heavy-duty zipper and a stainless steel track. Nylon elastic and thread are used throughout.

The kits come in small, medium, and large sizes and in short and long versions. The buoyancy capacities of the jackets range from 20 pounds for the small size to 30 pounds for the large size. (The USCG only requires 15.5 pounds.)

Suppose that you ask, "I would certainly like to buy one of these, but how can I meet USCG requirements?" The answer is: Go out and buy an approved, buoyant seat cushion, stick it in the boat, put on your life vest, and go.

The price for the complete kit is $21.50. Wildwater also has kits for making wet suits, spray skirts, and some other useful things.

The Deliverance vest by Stearns is fastened by a heavy zipper plus a waist tie. The bottom skirt can be worn up or down. The flotation is Aquafoam. The outer shell and the lining are of urethane-coated nylon

The Gatsby model is available in universal youth and universal adult sizes. It features PVC front and rear panels with a urethane-coated nylon outer shell and lining, and a zipper. Price: $28.35 and $30.20.

Also available is a child's vest called the Pee Wee, which is made in three sizes—for ages two to five, five to seven, and seven to nine.

For infants who weigh less than 30 pounds, the company makes the Kindergaard. This vest features a "float" section across the shoulders that resembles a set of football shoulder pads and would definitely keep a child's head above water.

For the canoeist who takes the children along, such vests should be considered "must" pieces of equipment. All sizes of the

7

Other Useful Accessories

Like other forms of transportation, the canoe and the kayak are an industry in themselves and have also created another industry which turns out products that will help make their use safer, saner, and pleasanter.

Some items (such as life jackets, paddles, and helmets—covered in Chapters 5 and 6) are not truly accessories but necessary pieces of equipment which make the craft functional and safer—as do an automobile's gasoline and seat belts.

The accessories cover a range that includes extremely useful products (for example, wet suits, dry suits, kneepads, outboard motor brackets) and products that may fairly be called gimmicks (for example, inflatable seat cushions).

The two most useful canoe accessories are the sail kit and the outboard motor bracket. The sail kit, although quite expensive (about $70 to $130), is a highly enjoyable addition. It can enable you to explore lakes, flat rivers, and bays without having to do much work. It can challenge your skill in high winds and at the same time provide you with a rapid means of getting from your lakeside cabin or campsite to your favorite fishing spot without having to resort to an outboard motor.

The outboard motor bracket is an inexpensive accessory (as compared to the service it will provide) which permits the purchaser to use his or her canoe to its fullest potential. It also enables people who for health reasons cannot undertake strenuous activities to enjoy most of the advantages of the canoe (quietness, speed, and so on) by using one of the many electric outboards on the market today. These little motors (generally of about two horsepower) propel a canoe about as fast as you can paddle it and create little, if any, noise or pollution in the process.

Kneepads are another useful accessory. They help alleviate the discomfort of kneeling on the canoe's hard bottom. They come in many forms and materials, but the type that basketball players wear seems to be quite adequate.

As for wet suits and dry suits, some thought is needed before you go out and buy one of these—first, because they are expensive, and second, because they were designed for a specific purpose, that of protecting a paddler going through cold water in cold temperatures.

Wet suits come in thicknesses of ⅛ inch, 3/16 inch, and ¼ inch. They come with full-length tops and bottoms or with "shortie" tops and bottoms. These outfits can be rounded out by adding hats, gloves, and boots.

Experience in winter and spring paddling in areas of western Maryland and Pennsylvania has shown that the full-length model, one-eighth inch thick, with gloves and boots and worn with a windbreaker over it, is quite adequate. It does, however, have a tendency to tear when snagged on overhanging limbs or brush, and for that reason we recommend the 3/16-inch model.

For those of you who are not "deep winter" paddlers, or who paddle in early spring and only need some protection from cold water, a "shortie" outfit might serve just as well.

The dry suit is just what the name implies. Unlike the wet suit, which uses body heat to heat the water in the suit itself to counteract the cold, the dry suit merely keeps you dry. It will not keep you warm.

A dry suit is quite nice in that it will keep you dry in the boat without the restrictions on movement imposed by the wet suit.

Another nice accessory—but one that is not really necessary—is the padded "carrying yoke." This is generally blocks filled with Ethafoam or urethane rubber which are attached to the center thwart of a canoe to pad the shoulders when the boat is being carried.

The cartop rack is another item that deserves a great deal of thought before you make your purchase. Such racks range in cost from about $10 or $12 a set for those with suction-cup feet to about $40 or $50 for a set of "quick and easy" brackets to which you bolt on the crosspiece. In between are a variety of offerings—such as foam blocks with slots to fit the gunwales, which then rest directly on the car roof.

Why is so much care in order in selecting the roof rack, and in examining how it attaches to the vehicle and the boat to it? Because if the rack and canoe fly off your car, there may be heavy damage not only to your equipment but to other vehicles as well.

Float bags are generally offered for kayaks and decked canoes. Although they take up a lot of room in a boat (as they are supposed to), the space they take up is space that cannot fill up with water. Hence float bags will make your boat a bit easier to rescue. Float bags are usually constructed of heavy vinyl material and are inflated by mouth or by a foot-operated pump.

Spray covers or "skirts" are as necessary as paddles, helmets, and life jackets when you are paddling in whitewater. They come in nylon, vinyl, and neoprene. In our opinion, the neoprene spray covers are the best. Generally, a cover or skirt is designed for use on a specific boat. For that reason, the best bet is to buy one when you buy the boat so that you can be sure it will fit and stay on the cockpit. To test, put the spray skirt on and sit or kneel in the boat and attach the skirt to the cockpit ring. Next, lean and move as you would while paddling to see whether the skirt pulls off the cockpit. If it does, don't buy it! Check some more, or order a spray skirt from the manufacturer of your boat.

Waterproof bags are necessary items if you are going to do a lot of "tripping," but they may not be worth the expense if you just want something to haul your lunch in. A good type to buy is one called a "battery bag." It is made of rubber-coated canvas and can often be found in stores selling military surplus.

Also available are rowing oars and seats, camera bags, repair kits, stretch cords, dollies, jackets, gloves, and many other items that you will find listed in manufacturers' catalogs and/or displayed at your local boat center.

Shopping for Used Boats and Equipment

Should I buy a used canoe or kayak? Are there advantages in doing so?

The answer to both questions is yes. You can get a sound, safe boat and save money in the process—if you go about it in the right way.

There is a similarity here to buying a used car: What *looks* good may not *be* good. So, just as you might talk to a mechanic before going out to look at specific makes and models of autos, you should talk to knowledgeable people before buying a used boat—to members of canoe clubs, to reputable dealers, or to people who build or sell boats, even if only as a hobby.

As with anything else that is secondhand, special precautions are in order because there will probably be no warranty.

Another very real problem—a phenomenon of our times—is the possibility that you may unknowingly buy "hot merchandise," meaning a stolen boat. How to protect yourself against that hazard is outlined extensively at the end of this chapter.

How much can you save? If the boat is like new or has been used only as a demonstrator, the saving might be no more than 10 percent. For other boats, it might run from 25 to 50 percent. You might even be able to buy a boat at 75 percent below retail. Such a boat would probably have many bangs and patches—and yet it might be entirely serviceable if the patches were well done and tight.

It is possible to buy a used boat for as little as $60 to $80. Yet most new canoes and kayaks today tend to range upward from near $300.

If a boat is a good buy and a demand item in your area, you will have to move rapidly to buy it or to secure the sale with a deposit.

Finding the Right Canoe or Kayak

"Where should I go to look? What should I

read? From whom would I do best to buy? Who could offer leads on the best boat for me?"

There are two purchase sources that do not require detailed discussion here. One is estate auctions, such as are advertised in newspapers. Another is the bulletin board of the neighborhood drugstore or supermarket. The odds against finding a used canoe or kayak through these two sources are high, so these sources are not worth much research effort.

From a Friend.   There are always advantages in dealing with a friend. These include the factor of mutual trust and the likelihood of getting a good price. Even a friend of a friend may have what you want. Such sources are very likely to let you try out your prospective purchase in the water. If you have little or no experience, the test should be made under controlled conditions, such as in a lake. If you are an experienced paddler, the test could be made in moving water.

The Canoe Club.   The canoe club and its newsletter (and/or its bulletin board) is probably your best source.

To receive a club's newsletter—and most such newsletters contain many "for sale" listings—you will normally have to be a member. The thing to do is: Ask about membership, and join. The dues are reasonable in most cases. In exchange, you will get the advantage of a wide choice and the chance to buy competitively (not to mention expert guidance later). Such a purchase could save a lot of grief.

Canoe clubs bring together canoeists and kayakers of many tastes and ages—who use factory-built boats, boats made from kits, boats that have been designed and built at home. The boats owned by club members will include cruising boats, whitewater racing boats, whitewater cruising boats, boats in many lengths, beam widths, and carrying capacities. They will include boats built from all of the many materials that are now being used. Also, stored in the club racks you will see boats that have been made by means of the latest construction techniques. Many clubs

have technical committees that evaluate such changes as they come along.

If a boat is fairly priced—or overpriced—you will find a knowledgeable club member who will tell you so.

Outfitters.   The outfitters that cater to canoeists may offer used boats in a variety of ways.

Some outfitters have bulletin boards where, for a fee, customers are permitted to advertise their boats for sale. Since the outfitter has a reputation to uphold, and may sell you some new accessories to go with a used boat that you didn't buy from him, he is careful about what goes on his bulletin board.

Boats are not normally accepted for trade-in in the way that automobiles are. However, they are often accepted for consignment sales, with the owner not getting his or her money until the sale has been made and the outfitter has gotten a commission. The commission may run about 10 to 20 percent. If the boat is taking up space hanging on a wall or sitting in a showroom, an extra fee may be tacked on.

Outfitters will occasionally close out their stocks of a line, or lines, of boats, and go to other lines. When they do, they often give discounts on the equipment being closed out.

River-Trippers.   The firm that rents boats for river trips, whether for whitewater or smooth water, or both, is a special type of outfitter. Such a firm is usually set up right on the banks of the river. There is a special advantage in buying from it: You can test the boat, or boats, in the best place of all—moving water.

The owners of such businesses normally have great expertise. If they say that a given canoe or kayak is adequate for heavy whitewater, it should be. If they say that another boat is not right for that purpose, take their advice.

At the end of the paddling season in a given locale, such businesses will sometimes sell out their entire stock of rental boats rather than store it. Then you will find a good variety of types and prices—especially if you are among the early buyers.

Canoes and kayaks are rented out by the

day or by the trip. Normally there will be no such thing as a rental with an option to buy. The owner may sell you a boat that you have rented if you ask him to, but the rental will not be deducted from the price.

Marinas.   Also worth checking are marinas where powerboats come in and are docked. The owners of yachts and fishing vessels sometimes have canoes that they keep aboard for short runs where they don't want to crank up the big motor or for trips into shallow water. These canoes often have low-horse-power motors mounted on them, and some-times the motors are included in the sale price.

Daily Newspapers.   Canoes and kayaks advertised in daily newspapers are normally listed under "miscellaneous for sale" or in special "boating" sections that appear in the classified or sports sections only one day of the week, frequently Sunday.

Classified-Ad Booklets.   City and suburban areas now have small-format booklets that contain nothing but advertisements of items for sale by private owners—including canoes and kayaks. Many of these publications offer the seller a good deal—he doesn't pay for the ad until, and if, the advertised item is sold.

These booklets are sold at or near the checkout counters of drugstores and super-markets. None that the authors know of are available by subscription.

In some of the booklets, the organization is haphazard, so that you may have to do a lot of page-flipping to find what you want. Even so, such booklets contain lots of items, and a copy doesn't cost very much.

One advantage of looking through these booklets is that what they advertise will never be very far from you. It may be almost next door, or at least in the same or a neighboring county or city.

Whatever you buy, and from whatever source you buy it, here are three points worth remembering:

—This book offers you a built-in reference for factory-constructed boats. Let's say that you have located a 17-foot aluminum canoe produced by Manufacturer X. Look under its listing in Chapter 4, and you will find its spec-ifications, plus the suggested retail price if the canoe were bought new today.

—The price of a used boat, like that of many other commodities, will be determined not by what the owner may have paid for it years ago but what the equivalent product would cost if it were bought new today.

An owner asks, and gets, $200 for a canoe that he bought 10 or 15 years ago. The buyer has a good deal because the same canoe bought new today would cost him $400. In theory the seller also has a good deal. He has had the use of the boat all that time, and he only paid $150 for it new. The figures indicate that he has made a $50 profit, but it is really a "paper profit" because the dollars he gets are worth vastly less than the dollars he spent when he acquired the boat.

—Condition and demand, not age, deter-mine the free-market prices of boats. Boats do not have the "built-in obsolescence" that model-year changes create in the auto indus-try. Old boats can be very good boats, and owners can ask and get a fair price for them.

What do you look for when you are buying a used canoe or kayak? This varies with the construction material and the type of boat. So let's go into each separately.

Aluminum Canoes

Check the overall condition of the alumi-num, looking for dents, holes, splits, and cracks. (Grumman Boats, Marathon, New York 13803, will send you free on request re-pair instructions for their boats and pamphlet *User's Guide to Aluminum Canoes.* The pamphlet, which is a good one, is also available from Aluminum Company of America, 436-W Alcoa Building, Pittsburgh, Pennsylvania 15219.)

Check the condition of the gunwales. These will usually be of aluminum, but they may also be of wood or fiberglass. The weight of the canoe is placed on the gunwales when it is being transported bottom up on a cartop car-rier. If the gunwales are loose, the rivets are probably loose in their holes; the rivets may further enlarge the holes and fall out, causing the gunwales to come off.

Check the seats and the seat brackets. Check the thwarts and their fastenings. The basic function of the thwarts is to keep the sides apart. Whitewater boats sometimes have heavy thwarts that permit them to be sat on. If there is any doubt, the thickness of the material (the gauge, if aluminum) should be checked to see whether the thwarts can be sat on. The canoe may also have one heavy, wider thwart—intended especially for use when the canoe is being portaged.

Check all rivets, looking for any that are loose or missing.

Turn the canoe bottom up, and look at the keel strip that runs from the bow all along the keel and up the stern. It should be tight, have rivets in place, and contain no bends that were not put there by the manufacturer.

The canoe may have one or more flotation tanks—air chambers to keep it, and perhaps also you, afloat if it goes over. Unscrew the screws holding the cover plates, and test the air chambers for leaks by filling them with water. If there are minor cracks or holes, these can be patched with liquid aluminum, which is better for the purpose than silicone.

Instead of air, chambers may be filled with a foam material to provide flotation. Or sometimes an owner who has had unusual difficulty in finding small leaks may have converted it from air to foam by installing the latter. This is all right provided that not too much water gets into the foam. The foam supposedly won't absorb much moisture, but the authors once knew of a boat that gained from five to ten pounds per season in that way.

The aluminum canoe is about the easiest of all boats to check out. Its pluses and minuses are right there to be seen.

Fiberglass Open Canoes

More expertise is needed to check the fiberglass canoe than to check the aluminum canoe.

Check the thwarts, the seats, and the flotation chambers about as you did those of the

aluminum canoe. You now have no rivets to be concerned about. The flotation chambers are best patched with auto-body compounds, mixed and forced into the hole or crack.

Look for patches on both the inside and the outside. If these are made with duct tape (also called silver tape), they are temporary and need to be replaced with permanent fiberglass patches. The patches should be tight, with no loose edges.

Next, check the boat's gel coat—or the outer layer that was built up from resin in the mold. It will be about $1/32$ to $1/16$ inch thick. It can develop cracks not only from bangs and scrapes but also from flexing and from fatigue due to age. If there is a crack in this coat, and if the fiberglass cloth was not thoroughly saturated with resin during the layup process, the glass fibers in the cloth will act as a wick and absorb water. Such a boat will be no bargain.

Some boats have gel *layers* instead of gel *coats*. On the outside, a gel coat looks like a coat of paint. With a boat that has gel layers, you will be able to see the pattern of the cloth from the outside. In this type of layup, the cloth is heavily saturated in such a manner that the cloth "floats" in the resin. If you see what appear to be air bubbles or dry spots between the cloth layers, this is generally the start of delamination, or the separation of layers. A boat in this condition may eventually fall apart. Moreover, delaminated areas usually become very brittle and will break readily upon impact with the shore, a dock, or another boat. In such boats, breaks may also occur from flexing the hull when the boat is being tied down on a car.

Now, check for pinholes. Have someone pass a strong light up and down the bottom of the boat from the outside while you look at the inside. If you see tiny light spots, perhaps in clusters, you are seeing pinholes. These are spots in the fiberglass cloth where the resin did not fill and where leaks may well occur. Pinholes can be filled with auto-body compound, but the compound may be knocked out by impact with logs and rocks. A boat with pinholes may be offered at a good price—but the labor expended in constant repair can offset the saving.

Fiberglass Decked Canoes and Kayaks

These are essentially built like open-type canoes. However, in place of a hull with gunwales and thwarts, three pieces are joined together: a hull, a deck, and a cockpit ring. Yet there are differences. The kayak is narrower in beam than the canoe, and therefore lighter in weight. The kayak will have a seat that is built into or is part of the cockpit ring. If the canoe has a seat, the seat will be in the form of a separate thwart or a separate piece of carved-out foam.

Check the boat for all of the things that you looked for in the open fiberglass canoe, including delamination and pinholes. You will have to put your head into the cockpit to do this thoroughly.

Test for tightness and integrity. Pour three or four gallons of water inside the boat and slosh it up toward the bow and the stern by lifting the opposite end. Look for any water coming out in the vicinity of the grab loops or elsewhere near the ends.

The deck and the hull were seamed together on the inside with a fiberglass strip or strips soaked in resin. Check the joint for integrity and for cracks. On the outside, along the line of the joint, many boats have a decorative strip of contrasting color tape. Ask to have this removed so that you can see the joint line from the outside.

Make sure that the cockpit ring (and the seat, if the boat is a kayak) is tightly fitted and well joined to the deck. You will have a continual leak problem if it is not.

When you buy a used decked boat, try to get the owner to throw in, or to sell at added cost, the spray skirt that fits it. This item is generally made from nylon or neoprene. It has elastic bands at the top and the bottom to hold it tightly around the paddler's waist and the cockpit ring and keep out water. Cockpit rings come in many sizes and shapes, so that unless you get your spray skirt with your boat, trying to find the right one can prove to be a frustrating search that may not end until you write the boat manufacturer.

Kevlar-Reinforced Boats

These boats are extremely light and extremely strong. Part of their great strength derives from the fact that they are put together with epoxy resin instead of polyester resin. Their initial price is so high that the price of a used Kevlar-reinforced boat may be equivalent to that of a new conventional fiberglass boat. You may not consider such a boat to be a monetary bargain. However, if you have a bad back or leg problems, the light weight of a Kevlar-reinforced boat could make it a bargain from a use standpoint.

ABS and Royalex Boats

Decked boats in these two materials have a big plus going for them: they are built as one unit, with no seams between adjoining parts.

These materials have a feature that is most unusual as well as desirable: they have a "memory." If boats made of ABS or Royalex are knocked out of shape, but not ruptured or cracked, they will often return to their original shape on their own.

One of the authors once saw an ABS boat, made by Old Town, that had been wrapped around a rock so hard that its ends almost touched. The owners got the boat on a car rack and left it there when they got home. At the end of one week, the boat had almost returned to its original form. At the end of two weeks, it had returned to its original shape, and it showed no marks from the mishap except for some scratches.

In looking over open canoes of these materials, check the gunwales, the thwarts, and the seats. These should be in good condition and tightly fitted. Check the hull, looking for damage or weak spots that could develop into cracks.

In looking over kayaks or decked canoes of these materials, check out the seam line. Check cockpit ring against the possibility of leaks. See that the seat, if any, is well fastened. Check each end of the boat carefully for impact damage.

A good rule for any boat in these materials is: If the hull is punctured, don't buy. (Why not? Read on.)

Only a very few manufacturers are using the true ABS. Other manufacturers are using Royalex. Despite some similarities, the two materials are different. ABS tends to be of very consistent quality—from one batch of material to another and from one manufacturer to another. The quality of Royalex varies with the formula, with the temperature used in molding, and with the amount of gas employed in expanding the foam core.

The problem with both materials is that they are difficult to repair if damaged—especially if there is serious damage, such as a puncture. Repair kits are now available, but making a good and permanent repair is difficult even when these kits are used. Fiberglass will not stick to ABS or Royalex. Duct tape, and even masking tape, will stick, but these are for temporary use only.

So here is a yardstick that you may want to use if you are considering an ABS or Royalex boat: If you are going to use the boat on lakes or on cruises down mild rivers, fine. If you are going into whitewater, find something else.

Strip Canoes

Well-built strip canoes are truly boats that can set the heart to throbbing. They are stunning creations—almost too pretty to be put in the water. Most of these canoes are designed for racing, and such canoes do not lend themselves to cruising.

Typically, the canoes are built of cedar or mahogany strips, about three-fourths of an inch wide and one-eighth of an inch thick, bent into place over a form and then given a clear fiberglass skin, inside and out.

Since nobody paints such a boat or puts color pigment in the fiberglass—seeing the wood is what it's all about—the condition of the boat will be readily apparent.

The thwarts and the gunwales are also of wood. There are no ribs, since the fiberglass adds enough strength to make them unnecessary.

Besides a general check, give the thwarts and the gunwales a special look for the condition of the wood and for secure fastening.

These are light boats. Few companies manufacture them. Most are home-built for marathon racing.

Canvas-over-Wood Boats

These are classic canoes and kayaks—likely to hold their value as they become scarcer with the years. Fewer and fewer of the skilled craftsmen needed to build these boats are around, and newer materials such as ABS, fiberglass, and aluminum have come to dominate the field.

The main manufacturer is Old Town Canoe Company. Canvas-over-wood boats were also built by Morris, but its factory burned in 1918. It is a tribute to Old Town, the quality of manufacture, and the pride of the owners that perhaps 2,000 to 3,000 of these canoes, each 25 or 30 or more years old, are still in use, wearing the original canvas. The owners of such boats give them never-failing care, varnishing the wood, including the ribs, and keeping the canvas well treated.

If you find an Old Town canvas-over-wood canoe with a good frame but bad canvas, you can go either of two ways. (1) Put a fiberglass skin on the exterior. This will detract from the appearance, but it will waterproof the canoe. (2) Buy a recanvasing kit from Old Town. If you need to replace any of the ribs, Old Town can even sell you replacement ribs.

You may also find a canvas-over-wood boat that has been home-built from instructions sold by an outdoor magazine. Sometimes—but only sometimes—will the workmanship in such a boat be good enough to establish it as a bargain.

Another type of canvas-over-wood boat is the folding-boat or knockdown type made by Kleppar in Germany and Folbot in the United States. This boat is essentially a rubber-impregnated bag into which a frame is assembled. One problem with such boats is that the joints of the frame tend to break down. Another is that the rubberized fabric deteriorates from mildew because it was not dried out properly. Such boats tend to be very heavy, with a single kayak perhaps running 70 to 80 pounds as compared with around 35 pounds in a comparable fiberglass kayak.

Inflatables

Inflatable kayaks and canoes are a recent development. These are designed for use on lakes or other quiet waters. They are made of a rubber material similar to that used in life rafts. They have the same ability to leak as a life raft, an air mattress, or an inner tube. Fortunately, they are easy to check—just blow them up, put them in the water, and look for air bubbles.

Inflatable kayaks and canoes may suffer if they are laid up and not used for some time. Like unused auto tires, they can suffer from dry rot.

Life Jackets

There is a simple rule to follow in buying used life jackets: Don't!

The life jacket is a vital piece of equipment, and when you are boating, you should always either wear it or have it at hand. In the manufacturers' pictures in this book, you may see people out in boats or kayaks with no jacket visible. (Remember that these are posed pictures, taken under safe conditions, and that they are not intended to steer you away from the use of life jackets.)

You will do well to spend a few dollars more and get new equipment, especially equipment that fits you well.

Used jackets filled with kapok are especially likely to be defective. The envelopes containing the material sometimes rupture, and water gets in.

Suppose that the person selling you a boat is tossing in a life jacket or jackets, that he has no use for them and will not sell the boat for less if he keeps them. In that case, you might do well to take them, to check them closely for fit, and before relying on them, to give them a good test in the water.

Canoe and Kayak Paddles

These are also often tossed in when a boat is sold. If they are, or if they are bought elsewhere, check all wood for a lot of black spots. If you find them, you are looking at dry rot. It is going to continue to make its way through the wood, and sanding, varnishing, and fi-

berglassing are not going to stop its progress.

Check all shafts, whether they are of wood, fiberglass, or aluminum. They should be straight, with the grip on the top of canoe paddles in good shape. Shafts for kayak blades sometimes get bent from being hooked on rocks or from a bad tie-down on a car.

The blade portion of both canoe and kayak paddles should be serviceable, with no cracks or breaks. Ordinary wear can be disregarded.

Watch Out for Stolen Boats!

Like autos, jewelry, money, and other valuable things, canoes and kayaks get stolen. One of the features that makes canoes and kayaks popular—their portability—adds to the ease with which they can be stolen.

Some of the things that you can do to protect yourself against buying a stolen canoe or kayak are the same things that you do when you buy any kind of merchandise. Other things that you can do are applicable only to the purchase of small boats.

In general, *watch out* if:

—The value seems too good for the price being asked. He who seeks a "steal" may be looking at just that—but in the wrong sense of the word.

—A serial number or some other identification that has been added, such as an owner's name, has been obliterated or has been made illegible.

—The owner wants to bring the boat to your house but has some reason for not wanting you to come to his.

—The owner cannot produce a bill of sale showing his purchase or is unable to give other evidence that he is the rightful owner.

—An identification plate, showing the serial number along with other data, is missing.

—A fiberglass boat has been painted over. One advantage of fiberglass is that the color is normally mixed into the resin and subsequently molded in, so that painting will not be required.

You should always ask for and get a signed bill of sale, showing the seller's name, address, and telephone number. True, the identification that backs up a bill of sale may have been forged, but by insisting on a bill of sale, you will have helped take reasonable precautions.

All boats manufactured in recent years carry serial numbers.

The serial number of an aluminum boat is on the ID plate. It shows the manufacturer's name plus the length, the weight, and the carrying capacity.

The serial number of a fiberglass boat is molded into the hull on the inside, sandwiched between layers of material.

The serial number of a canvas-over-wood boat is stamped inside near the bow, and perhaps in two or three other places as well.

Even boats made from kits will have a serial number, probably on the interior of the hull.

You can generally check at several places if you fear that you have bought "hot" merchandise or are about to: a local canoe club, the local marine police, or the U.S. Coast Guard. More and more states have set up registration requirements for cruising canoes and kayaks, and whatever agency handles the registration is the place to check.

You should be doubly alert if: the seller insists on bringing the boat to your home (note his auto license number if he does); he wants all cash and no check; he is reluctant about giving you a signed receipt and producing an ID; he suddenly offers a big price reduction from what he originally asked; he cannot produce a bill of sale or his own canceled check to prove that he bought the boat; the serial number appears to have been changed or tampered with in any way or has been damaged or obliterated for no explainable reason.

These precautions apply particularly when you are buying a canoe or a kayak from an individual rather than from someone in the business. Dealers take such precautions as they can against acquiring "hot" boats, though these precautions obviously cannot be infallible.

Here is a collateral question: Once you've bought your boat, how do you protect it against theft?

When the boat is away from the relative safety of your home or your canoe club, or out of your sight for whatever reason, you have a problem. When it is sitting on the cartop carrier of an unattended vehicle, it is highly vulnerable—as far too many owners have discovered to their sorrow.

When the boat is thus exposed, you can protect it to some extent by running a chain or a cable under and over the thwarts and/or the seat. The type of chain or cable that is molded inside of neoprene tubing is best because it will not rattle in transit or scratch the boat. If possible, secure both ends of the chain or cable by padlock, not to the cartop carrier, but to the *vehicle*. The reason for this is that a thief can take not only the boat but the carrier as well.

You still will not have provided protection against hacksaws and chain cutters. However, you may have slowed down a potential thief enough to make the risk unacceptable; and you may have narrowed the field enough so that only a professional boat thief will rip you off.

Another advantage of using cables and locks is that if a cable is cut, a rider in your homeowner's insurance policy will probably cover you. Such policies do not, however, recognize canoes and kayaks with rope tie-downs as being "locked and secured."

Appendix

The American Canoe Association

The American Canoe Association is the nationally and internationally recognized organization for the coordination of canoe and kayak racing, and it is the leading organization that is working to keep wilderness rivers open to canoeists and kayakers. Membership at $10 per year is open to all individuals. The benefits of membership include a subscription to *Canoe* magazine, low-cost instruction through ACA clinics, discounts at leading canoeing and kayaking schools, free vacationing at the ACA's private island in the Saint Lawrence River, discounts on a complete selection of books through the ACA Book Service, and reduced entry fees at races and special events. You should send your membership dues with your name and address to: ACA, 4260 East Evans Avenue, Denver, Colorado 80222.

ACA is a member of the International Canoe Federation, the Amateur Athletic Union, and the United States Olympic Association.

Recent Books Of Interest

Canoe Poling, by Al and Syl Beletz, National Poling Chairmen of ACA. An old way to explore streams comes back. Poling theory. Basic and advanced strokes. Stability while standing. Competition. New challenge in whitewater. Said *Canoe* magazine: "It is superb, well done and very informative." Twenty-two chapters, more than 150 photos. $4.95, including postage, from A. C. Mackenzie River Company, PO Box 9301, Richmond Heights, Missouri 63117.

Building and Repairing Canoes and Kayaks—A Beginner's Handbook, by Jack Brosius and Dave LeRoy. Emphasis on fiberglass—for initial construction and permanent repair. How to do emergency patchups on the river. Techniques of "skinning" old or damaged boats. Where to work; tools and equipment; finding and using molds; safety tips. Thirteen chapters, 134 pages, many photos. $4.95 in soft cover, from Contemporary Books Incorporated, 180 North Michigan Avenue, Chicago, Illinois 60601; in Canada, from Beaverbooks, 953 Dillingham Road, Pickering, Ontario, L1W 1Z7.

Canoeing, published by the American Red Cross. Paddling in fast water, poling, kayaking, canoe sailing, cartopping, portaging, competition, tripping, first aid. Canoeing technique with profuse illustrations. Many of the greatest names in American canoeing served on ARC's text-advisory committee. Said *Canoe* magazine: "A wealth of information at a bargain price. . . . It is 'must' reading for anyone who hopes to effectively teach canoeing." Soft cover, 452 pages. $3.95, published by Doubleday & Company, 245 Park Avenue, New York, New York 10017.

Index